escape routes

JOHANN CHRISTOPH ARNOLD

escape routes

FOR PEOPLE WHO FEEL TRAPPED IN LIFE'S HELLS

THE PLOUGH PUBLISHING HOUSE

© 2002 by The Plough Publishing House
of The Bruderhof Foundation
Farmington PA 15437 USA
Robertsbridge, East Sussex TN32 5DR UK
All Rights Reserved

06 05 04 03 02 01   10 9 8 7 6 5 4 3 2

A catalog record for this book is available from the British Library

Library of Congress Cataloging-in-Publication Data

Arnold, Johann Christoph, 1940-
    Escape routes : for people who feel trapped in life's hells / Johann
Christoph Arnold.
        p. cm.
    Includes index.
    ISBN 0-87486-919-6 (pbk. : alk. paper)
    1. Christian life--Bruderhof Communities authors. I. Title.
BV4501.3 .A76 2002
248.4'8973--dc21
                                                                    2001004749

Printed in the USA

The man who thinks only of his own salvation
is as good as a coal drawn out of the fire.

JAMES JONES, *The Thin Red Line*

contents

to the reader

I have just finished reading an advance copy of *Escape Routes*. I read it as if it were food, hungrily searching each page for help, healing, and comfort. Being in hell while reading it – my husband and I had just separated, and it felt like the ground had fallen out from under me – I found every sentence real, applicable, and easy to relate to. I especially identified with the chapter on rebirth, because that's what I've been seeking. And I can attest to the truth of Arnold's words: "How different transformation looks to someone who grits his teeth and opts for the full treatment." That's exactly how it is.

When I opened the book, I was overwhelmed with anger, fear, confusion, and other dark emotions – and a feeling of hopelessness that I would never be able to come out from under everything that's been burdening me. By the time I finished it, I had found peace, and the belief that no matter how dark my past is, it can still be redeemed.

Read this book, but don't just read it. Apply it to yourself. If you do, I'm sure you'll find the same peace and happiness that I did, and the hope that even in the worst hell, there is always a way out.

A. S.

preface

Call it life, call it hell: there's not a person I've met who hasn't been lonely, discouraged, depressed, or guilt-ridden at one time or another, if not sick, burned-out, at sea in a relationship, or just plain tired. Sometimes I know this because they have told me about their problems; sometimes I can tell just by looking in their eyes. (I've met people who were trapped in the most crippled frames, but whose eyes radiated love and freedom and joy; and others who, though attractive, looked haunted and weighed down by fear.)

It is possible to reach even the most burdened person – provided he or she wants help – but there are never easy answers. How could there be, when suffering is an unavoidable part of existence, regardless of age, social standing, or income bracket?

Happiness is elusive – Hawthorne observed that chasing it is as frustrating as trying to catch a butterfly – yet there are few of us who do not feel entitled to it. And when we can't find it in this life, we still hope for it in the next. Faced with disappointments and pain, many turn to a religion or organization that promises happiness in the hereafter. Personally, I cannot embrace a faith whose sole focus is the world to come. Like Rabbi Abraham Heschel, I feel that "the cry for a life beyond the grave is presumptuous, if there is no cry for eternal life prior to our descending to the grave." Nor do I believe that fretting about the future is likely to improve a person's chances of salvation. On the contrary, the New Testament makes it plain that our first and only task on earth is to love God and our neighbors as ourselves. Isn't that more than sufficient work for a lifetime?

When I told Maureen, a feisty 96-year-old I know, about my plans for this book, she said:

> A book on heaven and hell? I just don't know. I'm not sure it's a good use of one's time – to worry

about the afterlife, and where you'll go when you
die. It's probably unhealthy. There's plenty to do
right now, here on earth. You can find joy in the
present, real joy, through serving others – by helping them or easing their load. You can also look
out just for yourself, though if you do you will always be grumpy. You will never be satisfied.
Maybe that's hell…Now, I suppose if I were con-
cerned about the afterlife I would have something
more to tell you, but I haven't.

I couldn't agree more with Maureen: there's no need
to speculate about heaven and hell. As she herself implies, the dividing line between the two cuts through
every heart, and every dimension of human life. That's
what got me started on this book – the fact that all of
us have known some form of hell in our lives, and that
insofar as any of us find freedom, confidence, companionship, and community, we will also know happiness, and perhaps even glimpse heaven.

There was a more specific catalyst as well – the
birth of my grandson Dylan last year. Every parent
knows the feeling of relief when a healthy baby has
been safely delivered, and my daughter felt the same
when her youngest son was born. But she was also

stunned to see that his upper back, chest, left shoulder and arm were covered with large, hairy patches of reddish-brown welts. Though the doctors said that Dylan was otherwise healthy and normal, they warned that these blotches were likely to turn cancerous. In fact, the chance of melanoma was so high that surgery, skin grafts, and other risky, time-consuming procedures might be necessary. They said nothing about the social stigma of disfigurement – the stares, the questions, the cruel teasing of peers – but they didn't have to. My daughter and her husband were already thinking of that.

In short, though proud and happy – and comforted by Dylan's infectious laugh – his parents were worried about the future, and emotionally torn. Why *our* baby?

Coming not long before Christmas, Dylan's arrival and the nagging questions raised by his condition got me thinking of another birth, and the message of the angel who announced it to the shepherds: "Fear not; I bring you tidings of great joy." Which reminds me of something else Maureen said about heaven and hell: "There's little point in fearing the future. Why not spend one's energy loving others instead? As the New Testament says, love casts out fear."

In writing this book, I am aware that my ideas are not new. Some of the most wonderful insights in it are as ancient as the Hebrew prophets. Others are drawn from the lives of real people I know, or from people I don't know, whose experiences have been brought to my attention. No matter their origin, all of them offer hope amid the pain and hardship that make up so much of daily life.

The joys of heaven are often overshadowed by clouds or hidden in the most unexpected places. Yet they are always there, ready to be discovered by the seeker who has eyes for them. And once he finds them, even the weariest soul will see that the agonies of searching were not without meaning.

J.C.A.

loneliness

Without the correction, the reflection,
the support of other presences, being
is not merely unsafe; it is a horror.

GEORGE MACDONALD

Three weeks before Christmas 1993,
Wolfgang Dircks died while watching television.
Neighbors in his Berlin apartment complex hardly
noticed the absence of the 43-year-old. His rent continued to be paid automatically out of his bank
account. Five years later, the money ran out, and the
landlord entered Dircks's apartment to inquire. He
found Dircks's remains still in front of the tube. The
TV guide on his lap was open to December 3, the

presumed day of his death. Although the television set had burned out, the lights on Dircks's Christmas tree were still twinkling away.

It's a bizarre story, but it shouldn't surprise us. Every year thousands of people are found accidentally days or weeks after their solitary deaths in the affluent cities and suburbs of the Western world. If a person can die in such isolation that his neighbors never notice, how lonely was he when alive?

Forget about the Information Age: we live in the age of loneliness. Decades ago, single-person households were rare. Usually only widows lived by themselves. Nowadays, they are increasingly the norm. In a world where marriage rates are dwindling, children are cautiously planned for (or avoided by contraception and abortion) middle age is synonymous with divorce, and old age means a nursing home, people are bound to be very lonely. Imagine: only a quarter of American households consist of a nuclear family. None of this is to say that all was well in previous decades – it emphatically was not. But it is probably safe to say that loneliness has never been as widespread as it is today. How many of your neighbors or colleagues do you really know as friends? How many people in your church are just faces? How often do you turn on the television because you lack companionship?

Speaking of TV, its ravages on social and family life are old news, yet the average American still watches three hours of TV each day. With that in mind, the usual excuses for not spending time with children, old people, or friends – "I'm too tired, my life is too busy!" – start to sound laughable. Today there is much hue and cry about violence and sex on television. But isn't the habit itself of watching hours of television daily, with little or no interaction among the viewers gathered around the screen, just as harmful to our families as whatever content we're watching?

Then there's the Internet. True, it is different from television; after all, most of us use it to interact with others via chat rooms, e-mail, and discussion groups. I use the Internet daily, and it's a powerful tool. Yet when it comes to building relationships between people, the Net – though touted as a social technology – actually "reduces social involvement and psychological well-being," in the words of a recent scientific study. It's common sense. The time we spend on the computer cuts down on the time we could devote to a spouse, a child, or a co-worker who might be sitting right next to us. Even the best virtual acquaintance is faceless, voiceless, and disembodied, and cannot possibly replace interaction with flesh-and-blood friends. In short, while our dependence on technology may not be evil in itself, it is at best problematic. Though it conveniently solves superficial desires for communication, it waters the deeper roots of our isolation.

It's not as if people were content to be lonely: despite the lack of community, many hunger for it – though instead of the real thing, they often settle for the silly spectacles of commercialized pop culture. Marketers have long appealed to the powerful and unfulfilled need to "belong," and play on it constantly in order to sell fake versions of togetherness. How often are celebrations of "community" or other similar events (Woodstock '99 comes to mind) mere hype – gatherings planned to create artificially what doesn't exist naturally in everyday life? What feeds the craze for raves, where hundreds of strangers dance together for hours? The recent focus on the health risks of the drug Ecstasy, in my opinion, somewhat misses the point. What's more disturbing is the isolation that drives so many youth to drug themselves weekend after weekend and flee their parents' homes in search of a place where everybody is their friend, if only for the duration of a party.

It's true that in the last few years new kinds of community have arisen that we ought to take note of. One is the rise of support groups, which offer an emotional safety net for working through everything from addictions and other personal problems to events such as the death of a child or parent. Another is the grassroots movement of environmental, human rights, and labor groups that converged on Seattle in 1999 and Quebec in 2001 to demonstrate against the undemocratic globalization agreements known as "free trade." Lost in the mainstream media's version of the protests, which focused on "mayhem" and "violent anarchism," was the intense experience of building networks and communities that preceded these gatherings. After all, the thousands of people standing together to brave rain, tear gas, and truncheons were there for a reason.

A woman who helped organize for the Seattle protests told me, "The feeling of solidarity and community among us was incredible. Even though most of us
were strangers, we cared and looked out for one another. Our aim was a nonviolent one, putting into
practice the teachings of Gandhi and King. There was
a sense of joy and expectancy." When thousands of
people from all walks of life come together to share a
vision after years of creative networking, I feel great
hope for the future. Still, such hopeful signs are far too
rare to solve the epidemic of loneliness that is the
special curse of our society today.

The word epidemic isn't just metaphorical. In
fact, studies suggest loneliness is so hazardous that
people who are physically healthy but isolated are
twice as likely to die during a given decade as those
who live surrounded by others. What is the cure?
Surely there must be more to our cravings than can
be answered by the simple presence of others around
us – who hasn't felt lonely in the middle of a crowd?
Indeed, that secret sense of isolation is the worst
kind. Kierkegaard, by way of example, writes in his
Journal that though he was often the life and soul of

a party, he was desperate underneath: "Wit poured from my lips, everyone laughed and admired me. But I went away...and wanted to shoot myself."

Such desperation is a common fruit of alienation from our true selves. If it seems an exaggeration, recall your own adolescence. How often were you insecure or lonely, unable to measure up to all those people who seemed to have everything – people who were smart, fit, and popular? And even if you were well-liked, what about your hypocrisy, your deceit, your guilt? Who hasn't known the weight of these things? Multiply self-contempt a million times, and you have the widespread alienation that marks society today. What else is it that stops strangers from acknowledging each other in the street, that breeds gossip, that keeps co-workers aloof? What else is it that destroys the deepest friendships, that divides the most closely knit families and makes the happiest marriages grow cold?

Given our human imperfectability, all of us will disappoint or be disappointed at some juncture; we will hurt others and be hurt; we will be mistrusted, and we will mistrust. But all this does not have to be.

We may justify the walls we throw up as safeguards against being used or mistreated, but that does not mean that they really protect us. If anything, they slowly destroy us by keeping us separated from others and encouraging pessimism. They result in the attitude summed up by Jean-Paul Sartre, who said that "hell is other people."

Few of us would admit sharing this sentiment. Dostoevsky, a notable exception, half-jokingly said that though he loved humanity, he couldn't stand individuals. But all too often, our actions unwittingly mirror exactly that view. How many of us *really* love our neighbor, rather than merely coexist? How often do we pass someone with a smile on our face, but a grudge underneath – or at least a quiet prayer that if he stops to talk, he won't go on too long? And doesn't this lack of love contribute to alienation on a broader social level? Entire sectors of society have been made to despise themselves: the jobless and disabled, immigrants and the uneducated, survivors of child abuse and the chronically ill.

There is another kind of alienation, and that is the feeling of disconnectedness from the world we live in. Strangers to creation, we have succeeded in conquering nature to such a degree that we have completely distanced ourselves from it. In fact, our technological know-how has made us so arrogant that we have begun to tamper with earth's biological and ecological order, and are rapidly destroying the very planet we claim as our own.

How far we have fallen from our real destiny! If only we were able to break down a few of the barriers that separate us, we might not resign ourselves so quickly to the idea that they are an unavoidable fact of life, but open our hearts to the richness that human experience affords – both in the sheer miracle of our individual existence, and in the joy of meaningful interaction with others. Further, we might catch a glimpse of what it really means to be a part of this universe – this great community that includes everything from the tiniest clusters of quivering microbes to the unimaginable vastness of spinning galaxies and stars.

Thinking further along these broad lines, one might wonder whether loneliness doesn't have significance even beyond our physical world, affecting not only the human sphere, but the divine as well. Is it possible, for instance, that God created us to fulfill his longing for community – that is, because he was lonely? It may be that as much as we human beings need fellowship with God, he too needs fellowship and desires to be worshiped by us.

As it is, most of us rarely contemplate our place in the cosmos – or even in the human family at large. And the price we pay is not only continued isolation and loneliness. Gradually sliding away from those around us and into our own private worlds, we fall prey to greater and greater self-centeredness, egocentricity, and – in the worst cases – even insanity. As my grandfather, writer Eberhard Arnold, put it in a 1927 essay:

> Each of us suffers from separation and isolation. We are sick and dying, diseased to the core. But before we can attain health we must diagnose our illness – and recognize the extent to which we ourselves are the cause of our pain. Our thoughts are repeatedly bound up within ourselves; fundamentally, we are able to see only our own point of view. We constantly call attention to ourselves, and fight for our own advantage, for our own small existence.

The sickness of the world lies in this isolation of the accentuated ego. An individual who feels no pain but his own cannot identify with the world's suffering. He cares only for himself, fights only for his own existence, and seeks only his own improvement and happiness. In this way, he increases the suffering of others. He is a parasite that endangers the whole. He has severed himself from the reality and unity of life. He has cut himself off from the whole, and must finally perish.

In a culture like ours, where the most outrageous behavior is defended as an individual right, and the "virtue" of self-esteem is celebrated to the point of silliness, my grandfather's words may seem overly harsh. But we do not have to look far for examples that attest to their truth. Egocentricity has always driven those who believe they control the world, from Nebuchadnezzar to Nero to Nixon. The phenomenon is not limited to the powerful, of course, but is visible in anyone, no matter how ordinary, whose arrogance or selfishness cuts him off from those around him. We all know such people; we are probably all like them to a greater or lesser degree.

One person whose thoughts on this topic have especially intrigued me is David Kaczynski, a social worker from Schenectady whose older brother Ted is best known as the Unabomber. In 1995 David and his wife, Linda Patrik, grew suspicious that his brother was the man behind a murderous campaign of letter bombs that had perplexed authorities for most of two decades, and the author of an unsigned manifesto that ran in the *Washington Post* and railed against government, technology, and environmental destruction. He turned Ted in to the FBI.

Though David has no doubt that he was right in putting his brother behind bars (Ted is now serving a life sentence) he insists that his brother's actions were a fruit of illness, rather than evil itself. That view remains subject to debate. But in exploring it – and in agonizing over what could lead *anyone* to the sort of desperation that drove Ted to lash out against society as he did – David has come to feel that loneliness played an undeniable role:

> My brother's life and his message, of course, disintegrated into a tragedy – a tragedy for the people he harmed, and a tragedy internally in that he began to disintegrate mentally. I think the root of his

problem was to live in a world where he saw things going terribly, terribly wrong while feeling utterly helpless to do anything about it.

Ted felt that as a society we have lost a sense of the bigger picture, or of even questioning the bigger picture of who we are…We no longer live in a natural landscape, we live in some strange kind of world that is dominated by TV screens and radio signals, and it feels kind of scary, kind of dangerous when you think about it…

It's been a real, lifelong source of despair for Ted that we have lost so much of the intimacy that once marked human society – in terms of community, and in terms of acknowledging and honoring the spirit that lives in every individual person. He believed that we were becoming more and more like the machines that we have created.

Ted started drawing away from my parents in the early '80s, which almost corresponds with the time when he apparently started to plant bombs or mail bombs. The last time I saw him was in 1986. I visited him at his property in Montana. He had already killed by that point; of course I did not know that.

Whether he isolated himself because he was ill, or whether he became ill because he was so isolated, is a chicken and egg question. But I believe the one thing that could have healed him would have been to be part of a community. My brother had a tremendous sense of hopelessness, despair. A sense of community might have softened the pain for him and relieved the tremendous desperation he felt about his powerlessness to correct the wrongs of the universe.

against despair

Hell is yourself, and the only
redemption is when you put yourself
aside to feel deeply for another person.

TENNESSEE WILLIAMS

Just as loneliness arises out of our alienation from self, from people we meet, and from the
world around us, so also the process of healing must
touch all these areas of our life. Paradoxically, the
deed we dread most, unveiling our hidden self with
its loneliness and failings to another person we trust,
is one I have seen bring people right to the door of
freedom. The positive results of sharing are often

instantaneous: walls crumble as we realize that we are not alone in our feelings of isolation or guilt. Simply realizing that another person cares about our burdens can release us to see beyond them.

Take the journey of Terri, an army veteran I first got in touch with through an Internet posting. Wasting away from what she believes to be Gulf War Syndrome, Terri wrote that she had contacted Dr. Kevorkian about arranging to "die with dignity." I e-mailed her to tell her that because of her suffering she clearly had a lot to give to the world. We began to correspond. A piece at a time, Terri told me the story of her life.

Her parents were both alcoholics, and her mother, unable to cope with four young children, left the family when Terri was five. Her childhood was a nightmare of molestation at the hands of her father and older brother:

> I was raised in a fundamentalist church. When I went to my pastor and opened up about being molested at home, his response was that he was sick of my family and our problems. I remember sitting at the altar in my church, crying night after night.

As young as I can remember, I have always felt an attraction to those of the same sex. I was always a tomboy – you wouldn't catch me playing with Barbie dolls. As a teenager I felt guilty about my lesbian orientation, since Christianity told me I would go to hell. I longed for someone I could talk to who would understand me. But there was no one to trust, so I had to keep these feelings inside. Throughout my teen years I struggled mercilessly over my thoughts and how bad a person I was to think in such a way. How could God love me with the feelings I had?

She left home when she was fifteen "because I just had to get away." Then came a string of tragedies. Terri's close friend took her own life in front of her eyes. Her stepsister, whom Terri admired and who had intervened to protect her from abuse at the hands of her brother, was kidnapped, raped, and murdered. An uncle she loved and respected died. Terri says she "snapped" and tried to kill herself by overdosing on Quaaludes and Tylenol. She spent six months in a psychiatric ward.

Terri married twice, but neither marriage was a happy one. Both her husbands were substance abusers; both were a lot older than she was and physically abused her. In addition, her marriages never fulfilled her need for love, partly because of her own actions:

> Besides, even though I was married, in the back of my mind I really wanted to be with a woman. There were times that I went to bars to pick up other women in one-night stands. I was severely depressed and tried to kill myself numerous times.

During Terri's second marriage, the pattern of physical abuse, bar pick-ups, and depression got worse. Finally she separated from her second husband, and decided to go to nursing school. But first she joined the military to take advantage of the GI Bill.

> Already when I enlisted there had been talk about war in the Persian Gulf, and I knew I would probably end up there. Sure enough, as soon as I finished my training I found myself on the plane for Saudi Arabia.
>
> Our squad leader informed us that we would be joining a convoy into Iraq. We were already out in the desert when they told us we'd be burying bodies. I was shocked. That had not been part of my job description – I was a truck driver, not a grave

digger. But orders were orders. Two guys in the refrigerator truck were sent to pick up American casualties, and the other four of us went to collect the Arab dead.

We had to drive along the road from Kuwait to Basra, the "highway of death" as we called it. When we got into Iraq there were bodies everywhere. I have never in my life seen so many dead people at one time. Not even on TV. We were in the midst of the dead. Some were on the ground, others were in their vehicles. They were oozing blood from the nose or mouth. Some were oozing a yellow-green fluid.

We were responsible for burying the dead bodies of Iraqi and Kuwaiti soldiers. But we also came across women – mothers who were holding dead children. It was our task to remove the children, sometimes babies, from their mothers and bury them.

There were soldiers with heavy equipment digging mass graves, and we were instructed to put the bodies in these holes. In the beginning they gave us rubber gloves, but when we ran out of gloves, we used our bare hands. We wore the same body suits for four weeks. Sometimes it was so hot we stripped to our shorts and T-shirts.

In some cases I had to enter burned vehicles to retrieve the bodies. To this day I can still smell the odor of burned flesh. I'll never forget reaching for the head of a charred Iraqi soldier. Upon slight touch it fell off the body, tumbled to the ground, and broke into small particles, almost dust. I was horrified. The men watching laughed.

One day Terri and a fellow soldier took a truck to another unit. In the middle of the desert he stopped the vehicle and assaulted, stripped, and raped her.

I don't know why I didn't shoot him right then. I wanted to. But I had to get back into the truck with him. I couldn't stand there in the middle of the desert and wait for the Iraqis to come and kill me.

When I got back to our base, I told my squad leader sergeant what had happened. He did nothing. I wrote up a statement of charges against my attacker, but no one ever did anything about it. In the end I was told that the burden of proof was on me. The soldier could have accused me of engaging in voluntary sexual behavior, and then I, as a married woman, would be charged with adultery.

When our mission in Iraq was done, we headed back to Saudi Arabia. On March 20, 1991, I returned to the States. The war was over, but my own battle was just about to begin. I developed an infection and felt sick during the two-day trip back to Saudi. I was vomiting and had a rash as well as cramps. I began to break out in strange rashes all over my body and lumps on my legs and arms. When I first heard the term "Gulf War Syndrome" I realized that I wasn't alone. Other people who had been in Desert Storm were also experiencing rashes, achy joints, and nausea, and they, too, were being told it was "stress." This was a relief to me, but it also fueled my anger.

Terri believes that the strange symptoms that have completely disabled her are a result of experimental vaccinations and exposure to chemicals and radiation in the Gulf. She was sent from hospital to hospital and underwent various tests. At the same time, she was suffering from nightmares and flashbacks. She made several suicide attempts and ended up back in a psychiatric ward.

It got to the point that I decided I wanted to die with dignity, and I wrote a letter to Dr. Kevorkian. I heard back from his assistants, and they were going to discuss it with me. But that was just when Kevorkian himself was going to trial, so nothing came of it.

Terri received a general discharge from the military, and has since then become an advocate for Gulf War veterans. But it hasn't been an easy journey. Her health continues to decline, she's continued to battle with relationships, and her sexuality is a source of ongoing pain and confusion for her.

One important recent step in her struggle to make sense of her identity has been recognizing that God loves the wounded in spirit just as much as he loves those who seem to be whole, and acknowledging that he must have a purpose for her life. It has been a difficult step, for it has meant facing the roots of the despair and hurt that once led her to contemplate suicide: her alienation from others, especially those who had hurt her. She says she now realizes that, "in most ways I have shut out the majority of the people in my life."

Terri started by working through her "forgiveness issues" – restoring her relationships with those who had been close to her. She began to reach out to her estranged family. Amazingly enough, she even contacted her father, who had physically and sexually abused her as a child, and wrote him a letter asking his forgiveness for the hatred she had harbored toward him up till then. She says that although he never responded, her act of forgiveness lifted a weight from her own life.

After several months of corresponding with me, and with a woman in my church who was able to help her over a severe bout of depression, Terri and I met in person. We talked about the children in Iraq, millions of whom still suffer terribly in the aftermath of the Gulf War. Terri was horrified, and depressed, to find out how much the people she'd been taught to call enemies were hurting. These thoughts wouldn't leave her, and after several months she decided to travel to Iraq on a tour with Veterans for Peace. Travel took a lot of courage on her part: confined to a wheelchair, she's also still afflicted with nightmares and flashbacks. For the first part of the trip (as she told me later) she was miserable.

But the journey proved to be a moment when her healing deepened, changing the course of her life. While visiting victims of U.S. bombing, Terri met a woman whose child was killed in a January 1999 raid. She asked her for forgiveness for her part in the war.

The woman dropped to her knees beside Terri's wheelchair and kept repeating, "Of course you're forgiven...of course you are." In Terri's words, "When I asked that woman to forgive me, that was the turning point in my life." A few weeks earlier she had written:

> I think back to a couple of years ago and how bad I wanted to die. I saw no good in my life and no worth in my living. Today, I know of God's hope and my worth in this life. I want to live my life to its fullest, while trying to be a light for others who need to see the love of God.

Reading these words, we might think that Terri's story has a happy ending – and in a sense it does. But she knows that her struggle is not over. Like every one of us, she must daily renew her decision to fight her demons and work toward wholeness, both within herself and in relation to others. A disease of the spirit won't simply go away and stay away. But we can choose to turn the battle against it into a positive one – even into a source of strength.

It is often the achingly lonely person who revolts against injustice and seeks new ways. "If change is to come, it will come from the margins," comments

Wendell Berry. "It was the desert, not the temple, that gave us the prophets." It should be enough to think of all the giants of history who found their calling in solitude – Elijah in the wilderness, Zoroaster among the animals, Muhammed in a cave, and Gandhi, the withdrawn law student. These men did not fit into the society of their day and must have often longed for the comradeship of others. Paradoxically, their solitude energized them as they blazed new trails toward truth and justice. In their lives, loneliness resulted in a burning zeal – a fire that has illumined every generation since.

In sum, as Terri found, recovery from the twin scourges of loneliness and despair is not found by seeking to receive affection, but by active loving. When we love, the pangs that come at friendless times do not necessarily disappear, but their pain no longer torments us. Perhaps that's why there's an awe-inspiring quality to the loneliness of people who were so convinced of a cause that they were willing to die a solitary death. Their way of living and dying shows how little the cure for our affliction depends on what happens to us, since our fulfillment comes from choosing to love. Vincent van Gogh, who knew intimately both the agony of isolation and the joy of creative action, put it best:

> Do you know what makes the prison of loneliness and suspicion disappear? Every deep, genuine affection. Being friends, being brothers, loving, that is what opens the prison, with supreme power, by some magic force. Without these one stays dead. But wherever affection is revived, there life revives.

rescuing the past

Agony, which is not denied to any man,
is given to strange ways in children.

FLANNERY O'CONNOR

My childhood in rural South America was
marked by poverty and hard work, but also by an invincible sense of happiness and the security of
knowing that my parents loved me. My father was
strict, yet one of the warmest and funniest men I've
known, and aside from that, he seemed capable of
everything – taming a wild horse, making furniture,
building violins and guitars from scratch, and tending a garden that was the envy of our neighbors. My
mother, a teacher, was equally firm, gifted, and

warmhearted. But her defining trait was her energy.
Even with seven growing children in the house, she
found time to knit, make gifts (usually preserves of
berries she picked herself), and visit sick and elderly
neighbors.

Though my parents both went through plenty before I was born (after fleeing to England from Nazi
Germany, they were classified as enemy aliens and
forced to leave that country as well), I myself had a
happy childhood. In fact, until I was about twelve, I
never imagined that life could be better anywhere.

Adolescence changed everything. To begin with, I
had medical and dental problems that kept me from
participating in sports and set me apart socially from
my healthier peers. Then, when I was fourteen, we
moved to the United States, and my life as an out-
sider really began.

As if the jump from rural South America to New
York wasn't enough, there was the language barrier.
I knew German and Spanish, but hardly a word of
English. Like many immigrant kids, I found that my
accent and clumsy grammar were easy targets at
school. I lacked confidence, and the prospect of a

simple conversation was enough to unnerve me. The only boy in a family of seven, I always felt that I was the odd man out, even though my sisters were admirably kind to me. On top of that, throughout my high school years my father's work often took him away, sometimes for long periods of time. Not surprisingly, I was desperately lonely.

Obviously, there are worse things than such adolescent angst. There are millions of adults who grew up without the security of two parents; millions more who endured neglect and abuse. Still, my work as a counselor has taught me that the degree of hardship a person experiences as a child may not correspond with their woundedness as an adult. Further, because its nature and intensity may not always be apparent, the emotional suffering of another should never be trivialized.

It is often claimed that children are resilient, and this is basically true. As Dorothy Day once noted, their capacity to forgive outshines that of most adults:

> One thing children certainly accomplish, and that is…they go on loving. They may look at the most vicious person, and if he is at that moment good

and kind and doing something that they can be interested in or admire, there they are, pouring out their hearts to him.

Nevertheless, children have no immune defense against evil, and even the smallest germ of pain, hatred, or horror may infect their entire development and sense of self for years. Childhood is the first great battleground between heaven and hell, and its victories and losses tend to shape us in ways that later experiences will not. More simply put, a great part of coming to terms with ourselves as adults is coming to terms with who we were as children.

Psychologists and therapists speak of discovering one's "inner child," and in general, this is accepted as an important, positive, worthy pursuit. But what if your inner child is broken, wounded, or smarting? What if you're like Scott, a young man I know whose childhood was hell?

> My father, while physically present, was always –
> and still is – a complete stranger. I realize that this
> situation is by no means an uncommon one in
> today's society. Yet that doesn't make its lifelong
> effects any less real.

My earliest memory is of a physical and verbal fight between my parents. I must have been three or four years old. Because I "mumbled" – something that infuriated my father – I internalized everything I felt. Every time I spoke he'd shoot back at me: "I don't have time to sit here and listen to you mumble, go away and come back when you can talk so I can hear you."

I became reclusive, distant, and introverted, spending hours by myself, fantasizing. At school, even my little brother would defend me by fighting off other kids, because I would just cry and try to run away. I physically recoiled at the slightest hint of confrontation, often curling up with my head in my hands.

Punishment was unpredictable and harsh. For example, at dinner at a neighbor's house I goofed off. Long after I'd forgotten the incident, my father took me on a walk. We ended up in a shed out of earshot where he beat the crap out of me. Eventually I outgrew him so the physical abuse stopped.

Up till my twenties, he'd try to hold me under his thumb – or throw me off balance by making me acknowledge that I needed him, but keeping me at arms' length. I grew to hate a line often repeated to me by my mom: "Even though your father doesn't show it, you know he loves you…"

My mother was a hardcore Christian, and our house was loaded with holy cards, photos of the Shroud of Turin, crosses, and pictures of Jesus. I would flee in terror from these images. Many times she reminded me of this, leaving me with the conviction that something was deeply wrong with me: "You were scared of pictures of Jesus." When staying at friends' houses she would tell me, "Be sure to pray, because I have seen the devil in the room you are staying in." She treated nightmares as occasions for mini-exorcisms, opening up religious books and leaving them around my bed, or telling me to chant "Jesus" over and over.

There were normal times in between, but terror was the underlying reality of my childhood. While the boys I grew up with had dads who taught them about cars, sports, and life, helped them with projects and homework, and explained sex and girls, I had none of that, ever. The only "advice" I ever got from my father was once after he had got mad and hit me. He said almost tauntingly, "You have a lot of anger in you, you'd better get it out or it will come out later in life."

For me the most tormenting thing about my father was the dual personality he had, abusive at

home but with a friendly face to the world. While
the sham of our picture-perfect "family life" slowly
but surely strangled me, others seemed blinded by
it. In fact, everyone I knew saw my parents as
"friendly and loving." And while my father had
once admitted to me that he was "incapable of
feeling," young adults flocked to him, telling me
that he was like a "second Dad" to them and saying how much they valued his advice. They meant
well, I know, but it was acid in my wounds.

When Scott was seventeen, his father finally showed
his true colors in an unexpected public outburst at
church, and the family's respectability was exposed
as the masquerade it had always been:

> Something snapped, I guess, and after all those
> years of everybody assuming that my parents were
> such loving, thoughtful people – while I was si-
> lently screaming out for help – everything came to
> a head. My parents escaped the situation by mov-
> ing to my father's hometown. I found another
> place on my own.
>
> During the first couple of weeks I fell apart. I
> tried alcohol first, and when that ran out the really
> bad nights came. The first time, I just had a few
> beers with a friend. The next time, though, I drank
> alone, and I got this really dark feeling. A sense of

total terror just hit me; I wanted to die. I wandered outside, in the dark, only to be terrorized further by the tempting thought of throwing myself under a train on the tracks that went by the house. I panicked, and went back inside.

How do people like Scott deal with the hell of their past? One way, tragically, is by conceding defeat – letting old sores fester, and allowing the pain that wells up as a result to ferment until it is a poisonous brew. It's a devilish cycle, and one that will spin off new hells as long as it turns. It's also the cycle of imprisonment – of shackling ourselves to the evil we have suffered and eventually becoming one with it.

Another tack is nurturing a "positive attitude," and holding on to faith in the numbing effect of time. Both work, to a degree. Time does heal, and a hopeful outlook is certainly better than a pessimistic one. But just as hours of scrubbing cannot fully remove some stains, the best will in the world may not be enough to erase the marks of emotional pain.

A third way is to let go of the resentment we nurse toward the agent of our misery. This is easier said than done. For many people it is so difficult that it takes years, and in the interim the past may bind them so tightly that the way ahead seems barred. Still – and I do not say this lightly – those who go this route will find that when it comes to picking up the pieces of a shattered childhood, what they do has greater significance than even the worst that was done to them.

That is what Scott discovered. The years since he and his parents parted ways have been anything but easy, and yet in actively confronting the dark places of his past and struggling to forgive his parents, he has found release from the grip in which they once held him.

Like Scott, Nina knows the horror of growing up in a family whose wholesomeness is only a façade. To outsiders, her father presided over the perfect suburban household; to Nina and her siblings, he was a monster given to violent, alcohol-induced fits, and a dictator whose ability to inflict torture on others was matched only by the suicidal rage with which he sometimes turned on himself.

It didn't hit me until I was an adult what impact my father's violence had on my life. I somehow thought this must be how everyone lives: watching your father throw things at your mother, curse her and push her around, and hating him for it – but also hating your mother for "allowing" herself and her children to be the victims...

I deeply loved my older brother, who got the most violent abuse. Several times my father attacked him when his back was turned: once with a large standing lamp and once with a telephone cord that he wrapped around his neck. It was terrifying to watch, but I couldn't *not* look, in case my brother got killed. There were chases, too – my father running after my brother, and my brother falling (or being pushed?) through the big sliding glass doors. Once my brother pinned my father to the floor and began sitting on his stomach and knocking the air out of him. I think this was after he had hit my mother or something. My memory is screaming "Kill him!" Luckily my brother stopped after a while.

Some time later my father was forced into detox after a very bloody suicide attempt. At this point my mother left him and we got our own separate apartment. That was a happy time for me – until I found out that she had allowed him to come back and live with us. I could not under-

stand why my mother did this, but I chalked it up
to selfishness and hated her for it for years.

As I grew older I tried to forget my whole
childhood – the violence, the dark stuffy rooms
(we were not allowed to open the curtains on the
street side of the house because of the neighbors
seeing in) – by completely ignoring my father. I
assumed that everybody despised their parents, especially their fathers, so this feeling never both-
ered me; in fact I felt protected and nourished by
my hatred.

Nina left home at eighteen, went to college, and later
moved to another state, where she gradually found
her feet in a caring church. It was a long, hard road:

Everyone there seemed so healthy and happy, so
faithful and fulfilled, but I just couldn't embody
these qualities myself. I felt cut off, oppressed, unable to break out of my past. I tried to contort myself into feeling free and happy, and managed to
some extent. But it was a cold comfort and brought
me no real relief...

Several years later, after turning to a couple who
helped her unburden herself by sharing everything
about her past, including her own blunders and sins,

Nina found (in her own words) "repentance, conversion, forgiveness, and release. I was still deeply damaged, but I had made myself vulnerable and exposed
myself for what I was. It was clearly the beginning of
a healing process I never imagined possible."

Mindful of her parents' abusive marriage, Nina
still feared intimacy, however, and decided to remain
single. Offers came, she says, but she always de-
clined. She was convinced she could never be happy
in a relationship.

> Then, out of nowhere, a recovering alcoholic came
> into my life – seventeen years of active abuse, and
> only one year clean. We fell in love. Was I crazy?
> Did God really think this would work? Doubtful,
> fearful, then daring, we got married. The begin-
> ning was a roller-coaster ride, but God and close
> friends were always there – and the overwhelming
> sense that it was not by chance that I had married
> this man.
>
> He had all the same characteristics, weaknesses,
> and quirks as my father, but instead of succumbing
> to them, he overcame them one by one. Where my
> father had been arrogant and never apologized,
> this man was humble and always the first to say he

was sorry. My father lied; this man was honest. My father slept most of the day – this man worked out to keep physically and mentally fit. My father never did what he promised; this man's word was his honor.

My husband will always need to stay away from alcohol. But watching him overcome his urges and impulses is a source of daily strength for me. And the fact that we can talk – he about his former compulsions and obsessions, and I about my past fears – is no less than a miracle. Both of us are on the same journey to conquer our pasts by discovering where we are still crippled and by striving to help each other forward. It's not a smooth ride – but it's an adventure I wouldn't trade for anything.

Though just as revealing as any made-for-TV confession, Nina's story, like Scott's, is different from most in a vital way. Yes, the wounds of their childhoods were soothed by confronting them. But the real healing came when they decided to part ways with bitterness. Scott found a new lease on life by forgiving; Nina found it by making herself vulnerable and allowing herself to be helped. And ulti-

mately, Nina did even more than that. Rather than
merely escape her past, she has ended up helping
someone else out of his hell.

One final example I often ponder is that of
Malcolm X, who neither excused the blows life dealt
him nor let them embitter him, but used them as fuel
for a positive fire. When Malcolm was still a boy, his
father, a Black nationalist preacher, was targeted by
the Ku Klux Klan. Not long afterwards he was found
dead on a nearby railroad track.

The loss of Malcolm's father plunged the family
into grinding poverty. The social services office
claimed that his mother was unable to care for her
children, and forcibly removed them from her, send-
ing them to foster homes. Worn down by the string
of tragedies, she fell apart, went insane, and later died
in an asylum. Malcolm himself grew up and drifted,
and was eventually imprisoned for burglary. It was
behind bars that he first encountered the teachings of
the Nation of Islam, which he joined on his release.

Malcolm later left the Nation of Islam and rejected its theology – more specifically, he turned
away from his hatred of whites and embraced a fer-
vent belief in the brotherhood of man – but I doubt

he would have developed his legendary passion and
self-discipline without having been tempered by the
painful events of his youth. In his hands, the suffering of a childhood marked by poverty and racism
became a tool of conviction, and added authenticity
and depth to his courageous, prophetic voice.

Few people would claim that they are grateful for
the scars they bear from childhood. Millions never
overcome their pain, and suffer for the rest of their
lives. Still, stories like those of Scott, Nina, and
Malcolm X give reason to believe that the worst
wounds can be healed, and that the very weights that
once kept us from moving may strengthen us in time
and even propel us forward.

In losing our negative baggage – inhibitions,
grudges, and suspicions – even the most broken of us
can find the road to freedom, simplicity, and joy.
And that, ironic as it sounds, may be why Jesus says
that we must become like children. For those to
whom childhood was a fearful, terrible thing, such
transformation is undoubtedly a grace. But given his
promise that those who experience it will enter the
kingdom of heaven, it is surely an attainable goal,
and the best assurance of lasting happiness.

success?

Time alone, oh time will tell.
You think you're in heaven,
But you're living in hell.

BOB MARLEY

Gary, a friend of mine, was the black sheep of his family. First the seminary where he was supposed to make the family proud expelled him for misbehavior. Then he had to settle for a second-tier university because he couldn't afford Harvard. His parents missed no chance to remind him what a disappointment he was. So Gary resolved to succeed, no matter what the cost.

Soon a high-flying financial consultant for some of the world's biggest banks, Gary prided himself on never accepting a job that came with less than his minimum terms – a six-figure salary, a house, and a car. He boasted that it never took him more than forty-eight hours to find a firm ready to fulfill these demands.

Meanwhile, he had no time for relationships with anybody. He began to hit the bottle, all the while keeping up a high-pressure schedule. Inevitably, his marriage self-destructed. In the emotional turmoil that followed, Gary experienced a Christian conversion. But his real moment of truth came when, to his own surprise, he found himself neglecting his clients in order to save the life of a homeless man he'd found dying on the street. The hours he spent trying to find a hospital that would accept this uninsured, unwashed drug addict forced his eyes open. In a flash of insight, he saw a world beyond the boardrooms and luxury hotels that he thought made up reality, and came to realize what he had become: a slave to success.

A decade later, Gary now feels free of the fear of failure that haunted him for so long. He spends his

time ministering to prisoners and raising his children, and lives on a tiny fraction of his old income.

We all know that money can't buy happiness. Or
do we? After addressing one especially affluent congregation, I felt as if I'd just encountered an ocean of
human despair. After the service, when asked to offer one-on-one counseling, the stories I heard con-
firmed my impression. It's not that the well-to-do
have a monopoly on teen suicides, drug use, family
breakup, or hidden alcoholism and domestic abuse.
But there's a jarring contrast between the glitter of
success and the ugliness that often hides beneath the
flashy appearance of prosperity. That's why it's often
so excruciating for wealthy people to discover a reason for hope when things go wrong. They believe
that there's too much at stake to dare to take chances
on real solutions; they think there's too much to lose
in the leap of faith it takes to go from hell to heaven.
And in this they may be right, at least if they're un-
willing to lose their illusion of being successful.

We're always in danger of ending up possessed by
our possessions. When this happens, it is a sign that
we have lost our dignity as human beings and become

mere tools for wealth creation. Inevitably, we'll treat
other people as tools too. Strangers to our own humanity, we'll find ourselves adrift just when we
thought the good life was within our grasp. The real
truth is that money and happiness are incompatible.
Jesus said, "It is as hard for a rich man to enter heaven
as for a camel to go through the eye of a needle."

"A hard saying," Jesus' disciples murmured. It's
hard, because you don't have to be Bill Gates to
qualify as rich – not in the eyes of a malnourished
child in Iraq or a refugee family in Bangladesh or
Mexico. Relative to millions in the world, many of us
are the man who may have trouble entering heaven.

But what about the American Dream? Our country was founded on a belief in prosperity and upward mobility, or so the Horatio Alger myth goes.
But there is a canker at its heart. The bottom line to
the trophies we seek as emblems of our success – a
house we own, cars, a stylish wardrobe, exotic vaca-
tions, good colleges for the kids, or maybe a fast social
life at fashionable spots for eating and entertainment – is money. Pope John Paul II has spoken out
eloquently against what he calls "the culture of

death," which is the poisonous fruit of such materialism: "The values of being are replaced by those of having. The only goal that counts is the pursuit of one's own material well-being..."

The first to be harmed by this are women, children, the sick or suffering, and the elderly. Rather than seeing them in terms of their innate human dignity, we judge them in terms of their efficiency, functionality, and usefulness. Instead of loving them for who they are, we degrade them by measuring their worth in terms of what they have, do, and produce. This is the supremacy of the strong over the weak.

We are facing an enormous and dramatic clash between good and evil, heaven and hell, the culture of life and the culture of death. The low prices and buoyant economy that fuel our comfort depend in part on the suffering of people we don't see, in sweatshops and factories we prefer not to imagine. The deeper we look into our economic system's history of pillage and slavery, the harder it is to separate the canker in the American Dream from the dream itself.

Maybe this begins to explain why the New Testament so bluntly states that the love of money is the root of all evil. Drunk in a money-driven frenzy, our culture quickly tramples down those who don't fit the economic convenience of the moment. Wealthy pundits look at Third World nations and can speak only of overpopulation and reducing fertility. They ignore the obvious but wise reminder that children are our future and, regarding them instead as expensive nuisances, drive up abortion rates. In some quarters, pressure is mounting to offer the aged euthanasia rather than shoulder the cost of caring for them. In preference to providing drug treatment or rehabilitation for people with criminal convictions, many clamor to see them locked up for life-destroying long sentences, or put to death. At times, the culture of death seems to defy even economic logic: materialistic attitudes have cheapened human life so badly that many people would rather spend a dollar on punishment than a dime on prevention.

The culture of death doesn't just injure the invisible poor; it's lethal for those who are economically comfortable as well. If success is our main goal for living, what happens when it eludes us? Having invested so much of our time and even personal identity in our goal, can we bear to fall short? The terrible secret is that our ambition for the good life may serve only to doom us to self-hate, mental breakdown, and suicide – or that's how Tom, a long-time friend of mine, sees it. His father was a pediatrician, an attentive father, and a popular member of his community when he put a gun to his head:

> Dad's finances were still in the red even after re-mortgaging our large home and asking Mom to come out of retirement to act as his secretary. Meanwhile, I was enrolled in a small and expensive college in Maine, and Rick, a grade younger, was college bound next year. None of us sensed how heavily Dad's feeling of failure and money issues weighed on him.
>
> I have always felt that Dad waited to kill himself until he knew I was home from college for Christmas vacation. That way, I would be there to help the rest of my family through the aftermath. I knew it the moment I heard the rifle report. I think he had wrestled within himself, silently and alone, worried about what had gone wrong financially, and what life still meant to him. Dad must have felt lonely for a long time, since he'd only known success, and did not find a way to discuss his sense of failure.

When the police arrived they asked right away for the suicide note. There's always a note, they said. And there was – I had already found it pinned in his wallet and was reading it before an officer snatched it from me. The terrible thing about the note wasn't the message faded and on frayed paper: "Dear God have mercy on me. I do not see any way out of my problems." What hit me were the small pinholes shining through my father's last words. This note had been pinned and unpinned again and again, until the last time. How many times had he pinned it to himself only to be spared through some sudden interruption: "The kids are back from the ball game so early!" Or, "Who's there at the back door – the dog's barking!" Or, "Mom's coming downstairs – not now!"

Tom feels now that his father shot himself because he knew his family adored him, and he couldn't bear failing in their eyes. Tom's own childhood idea of Dad as a superhero – someone who couldn't be hurt – outlived his father in Tom's nightmares:

Even when asleep, I found myself at the mercy of powerful dreams I learned to loathe. In the theater of my mind, there were two recurring nightmares. It was only a question of which one was playing that particular night. One of them starred my Dad escaping with a minor head wound, as in all the Hollywood war flicks. He was fine, and the only sign of his gunshot wound in this dream was his white head bandage. It was odd to watch Dad going about the den and adjusting the Hi Fi with the bandage on, but – as the story went – at least he was alive.

The second dream had the same theme as the other: "Nothing can hurt my Dad." In this dream, Dad gathered the clan on the back porch and courageously broke the news: "Kids, in order to make ends meet, I'm sorry, but we're going to have to sell the big house." Right on cue, we kids would respond, with full understanding, "Hey Dad, that's OK. Don't worry, Dad. We can do that. We can make it."

Tom says he wonders why his father couldn't communicate with anyone about the threats eating away at his dreams of success and at his self-worth. Did he feel that he always needed to be the perfect father, strong, resourceful, and gregarious? Perhaps the legacy of his tragic end is this – the lesson that though admitting and embracing our failures is painful, the inability to face them can be lethal. "If we learn this," says Tom, "perhaps Dad did not die in vain."

How can we best find the way of escape? We can start by thinking hard about what we value. Do we put our faith in money and the material signs of having made it, or do we find our fulfillment in close relationships and a strong purpose for living? If we recognize the traps of materialism, what are the seductive distractions – the house, clothes, cars, and small luxuries of the good life – that we need to be rid of? Boldness and honesty are better guides than caution as we act to free ourselves to pursue our real goals. The process of passing through the needle's eye by reducing our possessions is a tough one, but it's the surest exit from the confines of materialism.

Another thing we must look at is our underlying view of success, for it determines much, if not most, of the goals we strive toward. Too often we think that by trying to be the perfect parent or churchgoer we'll reach our potential and contribute to other people's lives. By driving ourselves in this way, however, we painstakingly prepare our own catastrophe. The "perfect" mother can drive her children to rebellion (and herself crazy); the "perfect" churchgoer can forget the purpose of his religion.

Perhaps we're in greatest danger when the success we idolize comes in the form of humanitarian or religious accomplishments. It's easy to point at others who, by driving for perfection in the good works to which they devote their lives, end up narrowing their vision, damaging their marriage, or burning out. Still, it's harder for us to accept that our own noble-sounding justifications for chasing noteworthy achievements will enslave us, less crassly but just as surely as materialism will.

That's what Henri Nouwen, who left a life of academic distinction at Yale to become part of a community of disabled people, came to conclude: "We have been called to be fruitful – not successful, not productive, not accomplished. Success comes from strength, stress, and human effort. Fruitfulness comes from vulnerability and the admission of our own weakness."

Anyone who is realistic about human mortality will sense the truth of Nouwen's words. Whether we have weeks or decades ahead of us, our lives will one day come to an end. We all know this, of course, but what do we do with our knowledge?

Many of us do nothing. By and large, we need to admit that our lives are a series of squandered opportunities. It's tempting to refuse to consider this shocking possibility and to turn our mental gaze elsewhere. Yet we know we are empty. We suspect that the kinds of success we strive for aren't worth that much anyway. Our private lives don't express the joy and the love that we would like to think they do. The promise of our childhood remains unfulfilled; wounds of the past remain unhealed. We are scared of getting sick, of going crazy, of dying. Though painful, accepting the knowledge of our failure is the healthiest and most fruitful thing we can do for our spiritual life. As character Tyler Durden puts it in the unlikely film *Fight Club:*

> You have to give up. You have to realize that someday you will die. Until you know that, you are useless. Only after disaster can we be resurrected. It's only after we've lost everything that we are free to do anything.
>
> You are not a beautiful and unique snowflake! You are the same decaying organic matter as

everything else. We are all part of the same com-
post heap. We are the all-singing all-dancing crap
of the world.

This is your life; it doesn't get any better than
this. This isn't a seminar, this isn't a weekend re-
treat. This is your life, and it is ending one minute
at a time.

Tyler's rant may strike some as nihilistic, but it ad-
ministers a dose of vital, if brusque, wisdom. We
must hit rock bottom for recovery to begin. Acknowledging our failure need not depress or shame
us – after all, it's the common lot of humankind that
we are not who we're meant to be, and this ought to
bring us together.

The medieval mystic Meister Eckhart wrote,
"Love even your sins, for they will make you love
God more." Obviously he does not mean that we
should embrace evil. But he does mean that the
sooner we acknowledge our sinfulness, the sooner
will we recognize our need for healing. As Jesus put
it, "The healthy have no need of a physician, but the
sick do." And that's who he came for: prostitutes and
tax collectors, the blind, the lame, and the demon-
possessed. As for himself, he wasn't "good" at all.

He was a blue-collar worker who worked on the Sabbath, exposed the clergy, denounced his country's political leader as a fox, and wreaked havoc in a holy place.

Too often we do our best to hide our weaknesses and failures from each other by struggling to keep up a respectable front. Afraid of revealing our inner unhappiness, we build walls around ourselves to block out others. Why do we pass each other by, wrapped up in our own thoughts and fears? Perhaps it is because we are afraid to be seen for who we are. But as Jesus' compassion toward those around him illustrates, life's deepest fulfillment comes from valuing every human encounter, and showing love to everyone we meet, especially if they are lonely, despairing, or beaten down. What excuse can there be for not conquering our shyness in loving? As soon as we're free from our drive to earn, produce, and achieve, we'll discover in every encounter the joy of finding someone to love as we love our self. Such encounters do not vanish with time: they are immortal for us, with lasting value. As the novelist Alice Walker writes:

Our last five minutes on earth are running out. We can spend those minutes in meanness...or we can spend them consciously embracing every glowing soul who wanders within our reach.

sex

Love, I thought, is stronger than death
or the fear of death. Only by it, by love,
life holds together and advances.

IVAN TURGENEV

The story of Viagra is a modern morality
tale about heaven and hell. Available only since 1998,
this anti-impotence drug has already earned its
manufacturer hundreds of millions of dollars in
sales, and praise as a long-overdue godsend that can
alleviate the pain of countless silently embarrassed
sufferers.

The key to the Viagra story lies in the details. Impotence is clearly a legitimate medical concern,

though hardly as widespread as any number of more
familiar ailments, from heart disease to arthritis. Yet
even industry consultants agree that most prescrip-
tions are not written for people with real physiological problems. Rather they are being sold to men who
simply want (to quote a radio commercial) "better
sex, more often," or believe that the drug "increases
over-all relationship satisfaction."

According to this hype, marital bliss is only a pill
away. But it ignores the real statistics. For one thing,
impotence only affects a small percentage of the
population, and so it seems likely that the dissatisfac-
tion that plagues the rest has less to do with their
bodies than with burnout, stress, substance abuse,
and guilt over hidden fantasies, infidelities, and lies.
For another, over fifty percent of American marriages end in divorce, adultery is common, and to
many, "relationships" are not good things, but synonymous with betrayal and defeat.

Despite its touted magic, Viagra has yet to begin
answering any of these destructive trends. Indeed,
only a few weeks ago I read of a survey showing that
in at least one major American city, Viagra-rejuve-

nated men are leaving their wives for younger women. Perhaps that's the side-effect of the drug that ought to be getting the attention.

We live in a society that is constantly talking about sex, but we remain deeply impoverished in our understanding of what it can mean. And it's not just the pharmaceutical industry that plays off our obsession. TV producers and radio hosts, plastic surgeons, film directors, and publishers – all of them play off an unprecedented public appetite for more. The obvious result of all this has been the wholesale commercialization of sex. But it has also meant the gradual disappearance of true intimacy and the degradation of the erotic into the crude and banal. In the space of a half-century, attitudes that were once unthinkable have become commonplace, and what was once classed as perversion is now said to be natural and normal. Yesterday's porn, as the saying goes, is today's advertising.

Some people insist that negative attitudes have merely become healthier; and it is true that much of what our grandparents saw as sin, our own generation sees as freedom. But for many of today's teens, neither view holds true. They regard sexual activity neither as a sin nor as a source of liberation, but as a quick fix for loneliness and boredom. "Sometimes I think the whole world is focused on sex," says Jake, a fifteen-year-old, with a world-weary sigh. "There are nights when I'm locked away in my girlfriend's bedroom while her parents are out...and sometimes I think, maybe we could really be out doing something else besides this." And even those who boast about their exploits often live in quiet fear of diseases like AIDS.

We are leaving our children a world where the very dimension of human experience that was once regarded as the most sacred and heavenly may turn out to be the most hellish. Robbed of the chance to discover sex as innocents, they have little idea of its mysterious capacity to satisfy not only bodily cravings, but the mind and spirit as well. To them, reverence is a meaningless, old-fashioned word; lust something to indulge; a condom the only necessary precaution. But the price is often high: anxiety, self-hatred, confusion, and despair.

How can we rediscover sex as the wondrous, divinely created gift it is? How can we be delivered from experiencing it as misery? There are no simple answers; after all, the sexual sphere is always precariously balanced between grief and joy, fulfillment and frustration – between heaven and hell. But that should not discourage us. Rather than leading us to treat sex as a problem to be solved by moralists and prudes, we ought to grapple with its challenges and enlarge our understanding of it.

One way we can do this is to resist the idea of sex as a merely physiological concern. That approach, says German thinker Friedrich Foerster, is not defensible, because it doesn't take the sexual sphere's organic nature into account and results in an uneasy love-hate relationship with it.

To lump hell on one side of the scales, with the natural erotic energies of the body, and heaven on the other, with our spiritual selves, is an unnecessarily strenuous exercise. Besides, it oversimplifies human existence and flies in the face of reality. Writing of a fictional Bible school where this is done, Wendell Berry aptly describes the distortion that results:

> Everything bad was laid on the body, and everything good was credited to the soul. It scared me a little when I realized that I saw it the other way

around. If the soul and body really were divided, then it seemed to me that all the worst sins – hatred and anger and self-righteousness and even greed and lust – came from the soul.

But these preachers I'm talking about all thought that the soul could do no wrong, but always had its face washed and its pants on and was in agony over having to associate with the flesh and the world. And yet these same people believed in the resurrection of the body. Their own bodies were soft from disuse or dry with self-contempt. And those very bodies that they neglected or ignored or held in contempt, they expected to be resurrected and to live forever. And they thought this would be heaven.

Such dualism has very little to do with real life. Each of us is one whole, made up of soul and body. The first is housed by the second, and it is through the second that the first expresses itself. Certainly there must be a constant give and take: the body, for instance, cannot always have the final word. Abstinence and self-control are vital, and often the suppression of desire, far from being a bad thing, saves us from hurting those we love – and ourselves. Yet,

just as we are not ashamed of our mental and spiritual faculties, neither should we be ashamed of our
bodies and their sexual attributes – or of sex itself.
As John Donne, that great poet of both sex and religion, put it:

> To our bodies turn we then, that so
> Weak men on love reveal'd may look;
> Love's mysteries in souls do grow,
> But yet the body is his book.

When we consider body and soul in this way, as inte-
gral parts of one unified whole, we will not (like as-
cetics) see them as constantly at war, but recognize
their indestructible harmony and acknowledge it as
natural and good.

Jesus is a perfect – the only perfect – embodiment
of this attitude. Though the son of God, he had the
frame of a human male, and he neither despised the
human body nor shied from the physical or the sen-
suous. We need only recall that he provided a wedding party with wine and allowed a woman to dry
his feet with her hair.

Unlike Jesus, none of us is sinless or pure, and if
we are to appreciate sex without being wounded by

it, we must learn to nurture the voice of our conscience. It is never easy to follow the dictates of the
heart; in fact, if we have grown used to silencing or
ignoring them, they may be very difficult to per-
ceive. But no matter our upbringing, orientation, or
experience, each of us has a basic sense of right and
wrong. And whenever we heed it in the sexual area,
even the most troubled of us can learn its value as a
source of guidance and protection.

Clearly, the conscience is not an infallible indicator
of truth. In fact, a heavily burdened one may be so
weakened by its load that it is as good as useless.
When this is the case, healing will be a long and painful process, requiring self-searching and unmitigated
honesty. It will also be deeply humbling, because the
restoration of the conscience hinges on a disavowal of
the myth that the gap between our public and private
selves does not matter. It does. Even the most defen-
sive adulterer will admit to the strenuousness of leading a double life; likewise, a compulsive masturbator
will grant that whatever the secret satisfaction he de-
rives from his habit, it is always subsequently spoiled
by guilt. Even he knows, as Thoreau once put it, that

"there is no liberty worth having, if we have not freedom and peace in our minds – if our inmost and most private man is a sour and turbid pool."

Tragically, our notions of sexual morality are so distorted by the prevailing culture that many of us have never experienced the happiness true freedom can bring. People defend just about everything they do by explaining it as an answer to their need for sexual "release," but bondage, not liberation, would be a far more accurate description. Prisoners of desire, many people spend their entire lives gratifying their own urges.

What a different world it would be for them, if they knew sex in its original God-given context – as an expression of love and commitment between one woman and one man. Only in such a relationship can sex flower most beautifully and yield its best fruits: the physical thrill of orgasm, the deep bonds of emotional intimacy, spiritual union, and beyond that, the potential for procreation.

This is not to suggest that the goal of sexual intercourse must be conception, or that it was intended for the young and fertile alone. One of the most meaning-

ful experiences my wife and I have ever had as marriage counselors came through Lauren, a woman in
our church. Though Lauren was deathly ill, her husband still slept with her; they had decided to share the
same bed until her last breath. "We've grown closer
than we have ever been," Lauren wrote. "Here I am,
with only one breast, riddled with cancer – dying –
and we can still be together physically in the most
beautiful way. It is a rare and wonderful gift."

Obviously, marriage does not automatically make
sex ennobling. I know couples who have slept in the
same bed for years but complain of feeling miles
apart. If we consider the contrast between Lauren's
joy and the fear and terror of an abused wife, we will
quickly realize that a wedding ring does not guarantee tenderness and love.

Marriage is a wonderful gift, but there are greater
things; it is not everything. And as Ralph, a voluntary
celibate I know, testifies, life need not be any less ful-
filling just because it does not include intercourse:

> Though I was sexually active for years, it's been
> twelve years since I had a girlfriend, or mastur-

bated. Not that I'm holy or pure or something. But there's something mysterious about self-denial – it's given me a joy and fulfillment I never knew when I was sleeping around. I have even seen compassion grow as a fruit of it.

Jesus said that those who can accept celibacy should do so for the sake of the kingdom of God. He also said that in the age to come, people will no longer be given in marriage. So to me, accepting this is also a chance to bear witness to a future in which sexual energy can be absorbed and assimilated into something far greater and more wonderful.

That's a hard concept to swallow in this day and age, when millions look to sex as the highest pinnacle of human happiness. But perhaps it's the key to answering the anguish that results when such rosy idealism is unmasked as the dangerous myth it is.

Pain or pleasure, soul-murder or nirvana, ugliness or beauty, lust or love – sex can be anything we make it from heaven to hell. That is why, no matter how completely we have misconstrued and perverted it, and no matter how deeply we have been wounded in the process, we must never stop believing that it can

be fully recovered and affirmed. Indeed, as John
Stott suggests in his book *The Unforbidden Fruit,*
we must actively nurture that hope:

> I remember reading about a California shepherd
> who had a couple of sheep dogs. When somebody
> who was hiking in the mountains fell in with the
> shepherd, he noticed that the two dogs were always
> fighting. He said to the shepherd, "Which of your
> two dogs usually wins?" The shepherd replied,
> "The one I feed the most." In other words, our new
> nature will gain the ascendancy over the old only
> insofar as we feed the new and starve the old.

crucibles

The towing rope binds a boat, but is the
bondage its meaning? Does it not at the
same time draw the boat forward?

RABINDRANATH TAGORE

Though Diane grew up in a county that
has one of the highest rates of multiple sclerosis in
the country, she never dreamed that the disease would
affect her. She didn't even really know what it was.
Until she was twenty-two. Then it hit her, unexpect-
edly and so speedily that in the space of a month, her
legs, hands, chest, and back began to tingle, stiffen,
and go numb.

Even in this era of exhaustive studies and high-tech tests, researchers know little about MS. They can't tell you how long you'll survive, or predict the nature of your disability. Some victims live until old age; others decline so rapidly that they die within a year. Some suffer from weakness, others from paralysis. Some go blind; others become incontinent.

The one thing Diane's doctors could (and did) tell her with any certainty is that each bout with MS leaves its mark. Eventually most patients end up in wheelchairs, dependent on others for almost every aspect of daily care. Depression is common among people afflicted with the disease, and suicide is a frequent means of escape.

Luckily for Diane, MS hasn't wrecked her life. Six months after diagnosis, she's still on her feet, and as optimistic and radiant as ever. Not that it's been all roses:

> After I was diagnosed, I looked up MS in a friend's nursing text. It detailed all the effects of the disease – all sorts of handicaps. I started crying. Would I go mental? Would I die young? Would I live till seventy with some horrible disability?

A verse she found in the New Testament, however, helped her pull herself together:

> I opened my Bible and picked a random verse. It said, "My grace is sufficient for you; for my power is made perfect through weakness." I've never read anything that seemed to point so directly toward me...and it has changed the way I think about everything.
>
> Lately I've even felt that I'm privileged, because I've been forced to live just one day at a time – I really don't know what my future will be like. I guess that was always true, but now it's become real for me.

Especially in religious circles, it's become a cliché to talk about sickness in this way: to note that it is capable of bringing about inner growth; to suggest that it may even temper the soul and leave it stronger than before. Unlike most clichés, though, this one is not empty. Even Virginia Woolf, a writer known for her cynicism, was able to see the positive potential in disease. Indeed, she once wrote that illness allows us to experience "tremendous spiritual change"; that even a mild attack of the flu can bring "whole wastes and deserts of the soul" in view. "In illness," she says, "we float, irresponsible and disinterested and able, perhaps for the first time in years, to look round, to look up… for example, at the sky." Further, she notes that in contrast to other states, illness is the one in which "things are said and truths blurted out, which the cautious respectability of health conceals…"

There are grimmer aspects to illness. When Elena, an anorexic relative of mine, began to lose ground, her whole demeanor changed: her voice became a whisper, her smile looked more like a tortured grimace, and though she had once been happy and outgoing, she became angry and withdrawn. As her sister describes her illness (from which she is now recovering):

> Elena was thirteen when she was first diagnosed with anorexia nervosa. She seemed a most unlikely candidate. Some people appear to have most things in life going for them and Elena was one of those. Always popular, she was a natural leader among her peers and never had trouble relating to people. She did well at academics, but studied aggressively anyway, pushing herself to be the best.
>
> Elena excelled in sports of any kind. Her favorites were running and horseback riding. She had a

fiercely competitive nature. Caring little about her physical appearance, Elena would arrive at the dinner table smelling strongly of horses, her black hair rumpled, fingernails brown with dirt, sneakers untied. Her appetite was amazing. She had never been a picky eater, but dumplings were always the favorite – her record was nine in one sitting. So from the outside, Elena's life seemed to be running fairly smoothly. She was to start high school in the fall and already had plans to be a veterinarian.

During the summer of her eighth grade year things began to change. Elena became quieter and more serious. In everything she did she was more tidy, more helpful, more diligent. It was a slow change, and those of us who noted it chose to ignore it. School started and Elena became more withdrawn and despondent. Smiles were rare and the wild laughter we had so often tried to silence at the breakfast table was gone.

She was overcome with an intense desire to please and worked tirelessly. Only months before we had had to drag her indoors to set the table or wash the dishes. Now she was obsessed with preparing the whole meal alone, watching intently as we ate, then whisking the dishes away as soon as the food was gone. She herself rarely ate, always claiming she had eaten a big snack or didn't feel hungry. Her never-ceasing busyness irritated the rest of the family. "Calm down," I felt like saying. "Chill out for a second."

The weather grew cooler and Elena began to lose weight. She started wearing bulky clothes – sweatpants, turtlenecks, and thick sweaters – to hide her form, but her face still showed. Within weeks her skin, stretched over her cheekbones, became white and pinched. Her eyes grew hollow, strange wrinkles formed around her mouth. When she spoke, her voice was high and nasal.

I remember thinking, "This can't go on much longer. If someone would just yell at my sister, she'd snap out of it." But instead it only got worse. She ignored her friends and rarely spoke. It seemed she couldn't work hard enough or fast enough – cooking, cleaning, homework, errands. She wouldn't allow herself to stop.

Then one day in October her body shut down. She began vomiting and by the end of the day was too weak to walk. I suggested a shower – it might make her feel better – but she collapsed in the bathroom. She called me in to help and I was horrified at the sight of her. Every single rib showed, her stomach was shrunken, her legs pencil-sized, her skin sickeningly white. She vomited again, then wept silently, whispering, "I'm going to die, I'm going to die."

I don't think any of us could have imagined what was ahead – a fight for life so intense that it absolutely transformed her physically, socially, and spiritually. It left her unable to concentrate on anything for more than a few minutes, unable to allow herself to relax for a second, unable to relate to any of the people she had felt so comfortable with only months before.

She told us of the voices in her mind – very real, audible voices that told her how worthless, horrible, fat, and selfish she was. Nothing she could do seemed to silence them. Each day was a terrifying cycle – it seemed that the harder she worked, the less she ate, the louder and more insistent the voices became. There seemed to be only one thing to do. Disappear.

And so she shrunk before our eyes. Every aspect of her life became small and unobtrusive. She communicated in barely audible whispers, attempted to talk to us without words using gestures and sign language. Her handwriting, once large and sprawling, became barely legible characters using only the tiniest spaces on a page. The voices kept on, and she couldn't allow herself to be heard or to take up any space.

The battle inside her raged on, at times so intense that she was physically affected – her face would become white and contorted, she'd stamp her feet or pace frantically, then fall to the floor, crying like a baby. At times she became livid, attacking those nearest to her with kicks and slaps. Shoes, books, and alarm clocks would fly across the room. Then, "You hate me. You don't care for me one bit. You always say, 'Sweetheart, we love you,' but you don't really."

Or she would run away. "You won't see me again. You don't know what I can do to myself." Once she disappeared into a fog so thick that it was impossible to see for more than a few feet. Mom found her at the barn with her horse and held her tightly as she wept. "Mom, you have no idea what it's like. Every morning when you wake up you have something to look forward to, but I don't. My life isn't worth anything. It's no use."

She spent the afternoon of her fourteenth birthday in her bedroom, "praying that I could have cancer rather than this." That night she lay in bed, hidden completely under the sheets, and sobbed. "I can't go on fighting. It would be easier to die."

Sometimes hell is just hell, and no amount of talk can help. Despite wishful thinking, most people are not ennobled by illness; to be blunt, they tend to grow more – not less – obstinate and contrary, headstrong, selfish, and impatient. Nor does a clinical term like anorexia nervosa, while helping to describe certain facets of Elena's illness, begin to address the questions they raise. What about demons, for example, or other supernatural realities? Sensational exorcisms aside, what are we to do with recorded instances of possession? What about Jesus, who drove out demons – ones the Gospels specifically mention by name? Science can explain the symptoms of almost every disease. But it can't explain why a particular person is landed with them, and it can't make suffering go away.

Johann Blumhardt (1805–1880), a German pastor known for his wholistic approach to counseling the sick, points out that because the physical, emotional, and spiritual are so deeply entwined, the best answer to illness is the one that takes into account all three.

Beyond that he suggests this age-old, simple solution: "Through prayer and self-examination, seek
the direct intervention of God."

Blumhardt never taught that prayer would always
bring physical relief. "True faith," he said, "includes
readiness for a negative answer." Moreover, he warned
against praying solely in order to get better, insisting
that people ought to just pray and accept whatever
came from God. Neither did he compete with doctors or disdain scientific knowledge. As he said in
one sermon:

> The rejection of medical help, especially surgery, is
> completely wrong. It is a mistake to reduce prayer
> to a singular method of curing illness. Healing
> powers are simply lacking in our time, so why not
> make use of the help people can render one an-
> other with the training and experience they have?
> Rejection of such help springs from self-will and
> impudence...Moreover, Christianity knows abso-
> lutely nothing of healing anymore... Especially in
> the case of mental illness, most pastors cut a pa-
> thetic figure alongside physicians.

Still, his basic advice remained: "Trust in God and
pray confidently to him." And when collared by a

pastor who tried to pin him down with a compli-
cated question about the nature of illness and healing,
he replied, "My supreme maxim is this: *Everything*
comes from God."

Particularly in our day, that belief may sound extreme. To me, however, it is a vital recognition. For
no matter how much we may claim to know about
illness, there is always that indivisible remainder for
which medicine has no answer. Ultimately, we do
not hold the reins of our lives in our hands, and
knowing that should be reason enough to turn to
God for help.

Tragically, most of us resist doing this. As
Blumhardt once observed, "Most sick people would
rather drag themselves ten miles than search their
consciences or bend their knees." Yet Jon, a friend,
says such action is vital – and well worth the humility and soul-searching it demands. Recently diagnosed with non-Hodgkins lymphoma, he says:

> When I first noticed my lumps I hoped they
> would go away. I think a lot of people have that
> sort of attitude when they sense that things aren't
> right with them spiritually. But lumps don't al-
> ways go away, and nor do problems. If there's

something inside you that you don't like, you'd better take care of it.

They took a biopsy of one of my nodes not long ago, and since then I've been thinking that I could use a biopsy of the soul – to have everything examined, and to determine what kind of therapy I need. Because all of us go through periods when we know we're weighed down. And you have to be a fool to say, "I don't care; I don't need therapy." Because whatever you're dragging around could kill you.

As someone who has sat by the bedsides of many dying people, I can assure you that people like Jon – people who have, in his words, faced "whatever you're dragging around" – are far more likely to die in peace than those who haven't.

When you're dying, it doesn't matter who you are or where you went to school, whom you married, what you achieved, how much you made, or whether you were good at what you did. When you're dying, the strongest moral resolve may mean nothing. Faced with the mix of inner uncertainty and physical pain – and the fear, regret, and anguish that death's approach brings – even the most composed person may come apart at the seams.

That is why it is often said that at the hour of death, nothing else matters but our relationship to God. This is not something abstract. In fact, that relationship can be measured by very concrete things: the love we have given others, or failed to give; our dependence on God, or our attempts to steer clear of him; love, or the lack of it; humility, or pride – these are the things that will either comfort or torment us as we prepare to die.

That, to me, is the message left by Dan, a friend who died of lung cancer while I was writing this book. A few weeks before his death, his condition got so bad that the doctor gave him only a few more hours. He pulled through that crisis, and I asked him what life looks like to someone who is dying. I'll end this chapter with his words:

> I was a college phys. ed. and health teacher for eight years. I coached baseball and basketball, and I was also the trainer for the football team. Physical fitness was very important to me in those years – though looking back, I never thought too

much about it. We don't, when we're in good health. We just assume that our bodies will always continue to function smoothly...

When I first got cancer I had to come to terms with the fact that I no longer controlled my life. I had to face the question, "What do I do now?" I also panicked and needed support. I felt lonely and discouraged, and absolutely helpless. It was hell.

Later, Dan improved somewhat, and for a while it even looked as if his illness were under control. But it wasn't, and he continued to slide downhill. Reflecting shortly before his death, he wrote:

The doctors have told me there is nothing more they can do; it looks like death is very near. I've had to take an attitude to what is happening to me, and I've decided to fight for life, breath by breath, as long as I can. There are times when I've had to go on autopilot – I couldn't go on fighting; I had to hand it all over to God.

Each time I've done this, I've found the trust that God knows what's best for me. I trust him each minute, each hour, day and night. I'm not in control, but now that's heaven for me.

Twice Dan found himself in a state of absolute helplessness. The first time the experience was one of terror; the second, one of peace. The difference, of course, was as simple as his outlook. It's the same for all of us, regardless of our physical health: depending on the way we meet them, the fires through which we must go will leave us either scarred, or refined.

suffering

Perhaps this is why it is man alone
who laughs: he alone suffers so deeply
that he had to invent laughter.

FRIEDRICH NIETZSCHE

In 1930, three years before Hitler took power in my mother's native Germany, she was working toward an education degree. An idealistic, gifted student near the top of her class, she was also an enthusiastic participant in the freedom-loving youth culture of her day. But she felt trapped by the "educated neutrality" that she sensed smothered everything from politics to personal relationships:

People nowadays seem to approach everything with objectivity. It's hard to come to grips with it, but I think it's really cowardice. Nobody can grow in the midst of such impartiality. It just makes you stupid. No wonder people go to sleep; no wonder things so often come to a standstill.

My mother knew she wasn't exempt from her own criticism – she knew that much of the suffocation she suffered under was her own responsibility:

It's so hard to have no one with whom to discuss problems. Spiritual loneliness is the worst thing I know. Sometimes it reaches such a state that it becomes deadly and oppressive. Conflicts and difficult situations never find a solution; you just drag them around with you. Sometimes disgust and repugnance with yourself take hold of you, and still you carry on with the farce.

In part, my mother's words reflect the frustration of a young woman facing adulthood. But the feeling she describes of confinement – when our environment and our own personality wall us up within ourselves – will be familiar to many of us. In earlier chapters, we've looked at loneliness and how we can begin to find healing for it by facing up to its roots in

our lives. All of them – wounds from our childhoods, false promises of success, problems in our
sexual lives, sickness and fear of dying – imprison us
in the same way. Alfred Delp, a Roman Catholic
priest executed by the Nazis, wrote:

> The most salient aspect of an individual's life is
> *confinement.* He is limited by being bound to con-
> crete persons, to his wife, to his children, to his
> parents; he is bound to his particular job, this duty.
> And this not only hinders, but ties him up and im-
> prisons him.
>
> Sometimes confinement defeats a person; he be-
> comes small and stays small. He becomes *le petit
> bourgeois,* the little citizen who asks no more of
> life than his little daily round, his little pleasures
> and worries and the means of ducking out of every
> scrape as cheaply as possible. That person is
> beaten. His thinking and daring grow tiny, he loses
> the courage to make sacrifices, loses the eye for
> great things. Until one day the storm crashes in on
> his life and shows him that the great horizons do
> apply to him after all.

What is the "storm" whose bracing downpour will
rouse us from our slumber? For my mother, it came

when she realized her world was hurtling rapidly towards catastrophe, while "decent, hard-working people" preferred to focus on their little worries and proprieties. She found liberation by abandoning a secure career as the administrator of the prestigious private school that her family owned, and moved to an impoverished rural commune. There she worked as a teacher, and met my father. Both were pacifists, and staunchly opposed to Nazism. When he decided to avoid conscription by fleeing the country, she went with him. The day after they married, they exited Germany illegally; she wheedled a sympathetic official into renewing my father's expired passport by reminding him that this was a honeymoon.

Not many of us will face such adventures, and yet the need to escape our inner confinement is just as urgent as it was for my mother seventy years ago. And the key to freedom remains the same as well: rather than steeling ourselves against life's hardships, we must open ourselves to them – let them transform us.

Twenty-five centuries ago Aeschylus wrote, "He who learns must suffer. Even in our sleep, pain falls drop by drop upon the heart. In our own despair, against our will, wisdom comes to us by the awful grace of God." Could it be that we'll find freedom by looking suffering squarely in the eye?

For us whose high standard of living shields us from the harsher realities of life, this will not come naturally. Most of us have been insulated for so long that we are numb to the suffering of others – and even to our own. Our media-driven culture is partly responsible, as our power to sympathize switches off in self-defense against a barrage of murders, massive earthquakes, famines, and atrocities. What's more, our numbness anesthetizes us to our own pain as well: we push away reflections on our problems with self-esteem, relationships, and disappointment. Many of us flee from an unblinking view of human reality into entertainment or consumption. Paying to be distracted, we let our hearts become callous and are unable to see the world from another's perspective.

But materialism is not the only false escape from suffering; selfish and sentimental religion is a culprit that's just as guilty. When religion becomes a fantasy buffering us from life's harshness by telling us to ignore the present and worry only about the after-life, it has become an opiate. It's nothing more than a dangerously addictive sedative that calms our feel-ings of anxiety or guilt. Knowingly or not, pastors or priests whose motto is "once saved, always saved" are perpetrating fraud. They hawk an easy gospel promising cheap grace – and seem to forget that once we really escape the prison of self-absorption, we will immediately find ourselves among others in a wider human community for which we have responsibility.

Seen from a global viewpoint, such efforts to evade pain appear delusional. A few million of the world's people live in comfort, but three billion do not, and one billion of them are so poor that they barely have enough to eat.

Take Raquel, a woman my nephew met a few years ago while traveling in Nicaragua. Raquel raised eight children alone in a backwoods village which (like most throughout the Third World) has yet to benefit from the global economy. They lived in a one-room shack surrounded by an immaculately swept dirt yard. Her husband had left her, so the family had no regular income. Food, when there was any, consisted of rice and occasional beans and root vegetables. All the children were bloated by malnutrition, and most of them suffered from parasitic worms. School was out of the question, because of the requirement that children come to class wearing shoes.

In November 1997, Raquel felt sick and went to town for a free check-up. The doctor said she had a tumor in her uterus. When a local North American missionary family heard, they donated $70 a month for medications. Despite this, Raquel died two months later, without so much as aspirin to blunt the pain of the cancer that mutilated her body. Her children told the North American missionaries that she'd spent her last check on food.

What does the suffering of a Third World peasant have to do with our sense of confinement? Stories like Raquel's make us who are luckier weep. Such a reaction may be natural, but it is also superficial. The first step out of our confinement is to leave our tears and take time to look without blinking at the suffering in ourselves and in the whole world. In my visits to prisons, I am often struck by how – contrary to the pious sentimentality that insists that pain will purify – most prisoners are spiritually ravaged by their experiences. As one prisoner, Ahmed, wrote to me:

> What is prison? Death. It has become a nursery for the young, a retirement home for the old, a drug center for the addicted, a psychiatric ward for the mentally ill, a concentration camp for illegal aliens, a group home for adolescents, a brothel for the guards, a trophy for the politicians, a beacon of hope for the unemployed, and a massive industrial complex for the entrepreneur.
>
> The cell is designed to destroy the will to live. It is death by denial of the intellect. The steel bars, the steel sink, the steel toilet, the steel walls all work to destroy the spirit. They tell you that you are one of the damned, the doomed, the caught, the trapped. Your self becomes one with misery, and from this union comes a feeling of utter worthlessness.

Suffering like Raquel's or Ahmed's is anything but ennobling; it is soul murder. And still, as we've seen from the stories in this book, every human being is destined to suffer in some way – the millionaire and the socialite no less than the *campesina* or the prisoner. No explanation can paint over that fact.

The second step, then, is to recognize that wrongs can never be undone, the dead can never be brought back to life – least of all by nursing our bitterness. Some of my best friends, people with whom I grew up and shared wonderful relationships, have destroyed themselves through this sort of festering anger. Often it's easy to understand why: the inconsolable family of a murder victim seeks "closure" by means of the death penalty; a young woman struck by a fatal disease cannot face the "injustice" of dying so early and wants an accounting from God. Understandable as such reactions may be, the hell they create could not be harder to escape. When we allow ourselves to be overwhelmed by thirst for self-justification or revenge, we will become so enervated by our emotions that we have no strength left to pick ourselves up and move on.

Only when we are able to find release from bitterness are we ready for the third step out of pain: choosing to make our suffering fruitful by embracing it, and with it the suffering of the whole world. "Blessed are those who mourn," said Jesus of Nazareth. Buddhism contains the same thought in its Four Noble Truths, which describe that state of suffering, how it arises, how it ceases, and how well-being can supplant it. I learned to appreciate the wisdom of this teaching when I visited Plum Village in France, the community led by Vietnamese monk Thich Nhat Hanh.

Thây, as his students call him, has known suffering as few others have, and speaks with authority that comes from experience. He and his fellow monks accompanied their people throughout the horrors of French colonialism, the Vietnam War, and the Communist takeover. The lengths they would go to embrace the wounds of their people were seared onto the world's consciousness in the 1960s with images of monks and nuns who doused themselves with gasoline and became living flames protesting the violence. The American press focused on the gruesome sensationalism of immolating monks. But the furor drowned out an understanding of how their willingness to suffer on behalf of the voiceless poor was, to them, an act of solidarity undertaken in the name of hope and humanity.

No work of literature explores suffering so beautifully as the biblical story of Job. When Job demands to know why he has been made to suffer, his three

friends who have come to visit him in his sickness and
destitution tell him that it must be his fault: surely
God will not punish the innocent, they say. (It's an ar-
gument familiar to us from today's politicians and
pundits, at least in reverse. According to them, the
poor – welfare mothers, homeless war veterans, drug
addicts, and the like – only suffer because they're stupid or lazy. We're told that they have too many babies;
their culture is anti-social and prevents them from
success; their morals are inferior; they haven't shown
themselves to be fit for democracy.)

Job refuses to accept his friends' arguments, and
berates them for their arrogance. Finally God himself answers Job, showing him the wonder of creation and lifting his mind above the relative
insignificance of his own suffering. "Stand up like a
man," God tells Job, "and see how awe-inspiring the
universe is!"

Reflecting on man's power to choose his attitude toward suffering, even in the most extreme
circumstances, Auschwitz survivor Viktor Frankl
has written:

> We who lived in concentration camps can remem-
> ber the men who walked through the huts com-

forting others, giving away their last piece of bread. They may have been few in number, but they offer sufficient proof that everything can be taken from a man but one thing: the last of the human freedoms – to choose one's attitude in any given set of circumstances, to choose one's own way.

Few readers of this book will know what it is like to be a prisoner, or what real hunger is. But that doesn't take away from Frankl's point, as the life of Salvadoran martyr Oscar Romero illustrates. Although born to a poor rural family and apprenticed as a carpenter, Romero rose quickly through the ranks of his country's Catholic hierarchy. He went to Rome to study and then returned to his homeland to work as a church official, where he rapidly ascended the ecclesial ladder. Comfortable and pious, he toed the line conscientiously and kept impeccable clerical order. In 1977, at the age of sixty, Romero was named Archbishop of San Salvador. Many saw him as a safe choice unlikely to antagonize the ruling establishment.

It was a year of crisis in El Salvador. In a country dominated by just fourteen families who owned sixty percent of the land, most of the population was landless and economically desperate. Many peasants had joined the guerrilla forces fighting for a more equitable system of land distribution. In response, death squads and rightwing paramilitary groups affiliated with the government targeted the poor, whom they blamed for supporting the guerrillas. The campaign included killing off the leadership of organizations that advocated for the poor, mutilating or skinning the victims alive to drive home the lesson not to resist. In the two years following Romero's installation as archbishop, thirty thousand would be killed. Hundreds of thousands fled their villages and became refugees.

Romero had always felt deeply for the people he ministered to, and several times had even protested cautiously and politely in the aftermath of an outrage that struck those he knew. Yet for years he balked at holding government leaders responsible for the repressive violence that they allowed or ordered directly – he wanted to think of the atrocities as aberrations. In this, he reflected his outlook as a quiet and dutiful servant of the status quo. Perhaps he rationalized that God would bring about reform, or perhaps his obligations to the country's elite blinded him to its role in the suffering of his flock.

Either way, it took the death of a close friend to shatter Romero's illusions and shock him into a startling metamorphosis. Weeks after his installation as archbishop, a death squad murdered the activist Jesuit Rutilio Grande, along with two young companions. Rutilio's death changed Romero completely. At the funeral mass, with the plaza full and overflowing, Romero did what he had never done before, despite his good intentions: he identified with his people and their suffering. Inocencio Alas describes what happened as the archbishop addressed the grief-stricken crowd of 100,000:

> As the Mass began, I noticed that Monsignor Romero was sweating, pale and nervous. And when he began the homily, it seemed slow to me, as if he was reluctant to go through the door of history that was opening up for him. But after about five minutes, I felt the Holy Spirit descend upon him. When he mentioned the name of Rutilio, thousands exploded into applause and you could see him grow stronger.

It was then that he crossed the threshold. He went through the door. There is baptism by water, and there is baptism by blood. But there is also baptism by the people.

After this experience, Romero changed from a timid functionary to a prophet. In his Sunday sermons, which were broadcast nationally, he denounced the greed and cruelty of the Salvadoran oligarchy and comforted the poor who made up most of his congregation. While calling for an end to violence on all sides, he never ceased to denounce the "structural sin" of a political and economic regime that oppressed the Salvadoran people in the name of capitalism and development:

> One could say of suffering what the Lord said of temptation: "Temptation indeed must come, but woe to the one through whom temptation comes!" Suffering is something inherent to our very nature, but to cause to suffer is criminal.
>
> *May 1978*

Unfortunately, brothers and sisters, we are the product of a spiritualized, individualistic education. We were taught: Try to save your soul and

don't worry about the rest. We told the suffering:
Be patient, heaven will follow, hang on.

No, that's not right, that's not salvation! The
salvation that Christ brings is salvation from every
bondage that oppresses human beings.

September 1979

We must save not the soul at the hour of death but
the person living in history. *July 1977*

As his worried supporters predicted, Romero quickly
became an object of slander and attack by those who
felt threatened by change. His radio station was
bombed, his priests harassed and killed, and his
churches vandalized. Three years after he became
archbishop, an assassin gunned him down as he celebrated Mass in the chapel of a cancer hospital.

Romero paid a terrible price for speaking truth to
power, but his death did not silence him. In fact, it
only amplified his voice. United (and thus strength-
ened) in their grief, his listeners took up their slain
leader's challenge to become "God's microphones"
and spread his message with increased fervor. That
message is summed up by socialist Eugene Debs,
who famously said:

Years ago I recognized my kinship with all living
human beings, and I made up my mind that I was
not one bit better than the meanest person on
earth. I said then, and I say it now, that while there
is a lower class, I am in it; while there is a criminal
element, I am of it; and while there is a soul in
prison, I am not free.

When we approach the suffering of others in this
way – by making it our own – we will find that, far
from defeating us, it will rouse us to compassion
(which incidentally means "suffering with") and
community with the poor. Moreover, we will find
that through solidarity, their hells, even if not completely overcome, can be seeded with love and hope
for the future.

rebirth

As long as you run from it – this "die and become" – you'll remain a sad wanderer on a dark earth.

J . W . V O N G O E T H E

We must change, or die. That is not only a biological fact, but a truth that holds the key to solving the great riddle of heaven and hell in our personal lives. Circumstances can't always be changed; other people, even if we may try to influence them, are still other people; the future is impossible to predict – even tomorrow is a mystery. In short, our best efforts cannot make heaven out of hell. But there is one thing we can do, and that is choose – to be selfish or selfless;

to burn with lust or with love; to defend our power or dismantle it. And that is why, instead of taking on the futile task of trying to change the whole world, we must, as Gandhi once advised, *be* the change we wish to see in it.

Real transformation is the opposite of self-improvement. It is one thing, for example, to spruce up an old wall by covering it with a new coat of paint; quite another to check for dry rot or termites and replace every damaged board. The cosmetic solution costs less, at least upfront, whereas the structural one, which requires far greater changes, also requires far more labor and time. But if that is what is needed, that is what must be done. Even if the new paint is shiny, the surface will soon prove itself insufficient to save the wall, and in the end, more will be lost than was temporarily saved.

As with the house, so with each of us. We can – as today's advertisers seem to have successfully seduced our generation into doing – spend the greater part of our lives repainting ourselves. Upgrading our computer, replacing the old car, shedding those extra pounds, going to the hairstylist to try the newest

look. Deep down, however, we all know that none of
these changes can bring lasting happiness. Deep
down, all of us sense that to some extent, the hells of
our lives are related to the brokenness of our own
hearts and minds, and that this brokenness is the
most vital thing we must examine and fix.

How we go about doing this is another story, for
knowing that a problem exists does not mean knowing how to solve it. We are by nature divided; our
souls are fissured, and we cannot bind or heal them
any more than the victim of heart disease can carry
out surgery on himself. And thus our transformation
depends not only on us, but on another power, and
on our willingness to submit to it, just as the patient
submits to the surgeon's knife.

Because we fear pain (who looks forward to surgery?) most of us do everything we can to avoid it.
And not only literally. To be inwardly cut to the
quick – to have one's false fronts torn away and the
lies behind them exposed, to have one's rough edges
chipped away and one's ego cut down to size, to be
"pruned," as the Gospels put it – simply is a painful
thing.

That's why we often settle for more convenient, more comfortable ways to change. We aim to fine-tune our marriages, improve relationships at work. We work at being a better team player, a better listener, parent, or friend. We choose something we don't like about ourselves and resolve to do away with it, or at very least change it. But no matter how many such timid efforts we make, they will not help us any more than painkillers, which suppress symptoms but do nothing to truly combat disease. They cannot bring us the much greater relief that comes from having signed up for surgery, and from being able to emerge after it with a clean bill of health.

How different transformation looks to someone who grits his teeth and opts for the full treatment! Such a person knows the exhilaration of undergoing a thorough upheaval, and even if he later reverts to his old self – to weariness, boredom, sickness, or sin – he never forgets the experience so completely that he won't long for it again. To quote the poet John Donne, who pleads God to "batter" him and thus renew his soul:

Batter my heart, three-personed God; for you
As yet but knock, breathe, shine,
    and seek to mend;
That I may rise and stand;
    o'erthrow me and bend
Your force to break, blow, burn
    and make me new...
Take me to you, imprison me, for I
Except you enthrall me, never shall be free,
Nor ever chaste, except you ravish me.

Violent as it is, this imagery does not describe the full cost of renewal, which includes not only surgery and its attendant "battering" of the heart, but the willingness to die. Donne touches on it, with the word "burn" – but for true rebirth to happen we must be more than seared. We must be burned away completely, so that nothing is left of us, and an entirely new being may come out of the ashes, like the legendary phoenix that rises from its own funeral pyre.

Or, to use a more familiar image from the natural world, we must undergo the same full-fledged metamorphosis as that of a caterpillar before it becomes a butterfly. Inside its chrysalis, a caterpillar loses all of its defining characteristics: its skin color, shape, mouth, and legs. Even its internal organs and systems are altered during the pupal stage, and its appetites and habits as well. It loses *everything* that once made up its identity. It ceases to exist as a caterpillar. But that is not all. In submitting to the destruction of its old body, it is no longer confined to crawling on the underside of a leaf, but captures the eye with its beauty and ability to flutter and float and soar. Whereas previously it could not reproduce, it can now mate and lay eggs: its reincarnation allows it to bear fruit.

What does it mean to "die," be transformed, and experience rebirth? First and foremost, I believe it means letting ourselves be dismantled – not partially, but completely. That, to me, is the crucial first step – giving up our dreams and ambitions, our worries and fears; yielding control over our social, political, and economic agendas; surrendering our most personal plans; even revealing our darkest secrets.

Equally vital is letting go of our goodness. Not surprisingly, that is difficult. In fact, having talked with countless people at critical moments in their lives, I've found that this is often the biggest sticking point. We all want to change, to become better people, to get rid of the negative baggage we drag after ourselves. But when it comes down to the brass tacks, most of us are just as eager to preserve every inch of our old selves, or at least our good parts. Having gladly dropped everything we didn't like about ourselves, we still cling desperately to the rest, refusing to believe that it might be tainted, and hoping that it can still be rescued. Yet the fact is that even the most sincerely held virtue can be a great obstacle to transformation. That is because a subjective view of our own goodness is rarely in line with reality; that is to say, few of us are really as pure as we might imagine ourselves to be.

Simply put, rebirth is impossible for those who are in love with themselves in any way, and that goes for a "religious" person as much as anyone else. Confidence is one thing, of course, and no one can truly live or blossom without it. But the self-love of complacency – the sort that leads people to talk about how they are "saved" because they were "born again" (or how they are "enlightened" because they have "seen the light") – is quite another. In fact, it seems to me

that those who claim such things are among the worst
enemies of rebirth, if only because their smugness is
often coupled with the assurance that the rest of the
world is damned. Maybe that is why Jesus reserved
his harshest words for his most pious countrymen –
rebuking them as a "brood of vipers" and comparing
them to "whitewashed tombs." It is surely why he
also warned them – and us – that "whoever saves his
life will lose it; and whoever loses his life will save it."

There is another ingredient to finding new life,
other than merely "letting go," and that is repenting.
Unfortunately, to many, the word implies hellfire
and brimstone. Actually, repentance is just another
word for remorse, or, to paraphrase C. S. Lewis, for
laying down our arms and surrendering, saying
we're sorry, realizing we're on the wrong track, and
moving full speed astern. Repentance, he says, is
"the only way out of a hole."

Naturally there are times when saying sorry is insufficient, and when there is no way to cleanse oneself
except by submitting to the heartache of shame and
humiliation. But even if such torment has a place, it is
never the goal of true repentance, and to wallow in it

by beating oneself up repeatedly is futile. In the words of Yitzhak Meir, a Polish rabbi:

> Turn muck over and over, it still remains muck, and no good can come of it. Therefore beware of contemplating your own evil too long. For as long as your thoughts are there, so also is your soul – and if you let it sink too deeply, it may not be able to extricate itself and repent.
>
> If you have sinned much, balance it by doing much good. So resolve today, from the depth of your heart and in a joyful mood, to abstain from sin and to do good. Say the prayer "For the Sin," but do not dwell on it. Meditate preferably on the prayer, "And Thou, O Lord, shalt reign."

On its own, in other words, self-contempt is useless. Having said that, I still believe that remorse is the natural response of a healthy spiritual immune system taking action to reject and destroy a source of disease. Without repentance, we can't realize the pain we cause others, and God, through our failings and sins. With it, we will know that pain, but also the freedom that comes from taking stock, facing up, turning around, and moving on. In short, repentance is the catapult that first yanks us downward and backward, but then shoots us upward and forward, right out of hell. Grace, a woman in my church, has a story that illustrates this well:

> Up to the age of sixteen, I was an average girl, alternating between wanting to be treated like an adult and claiming childhood status to escape responsibility. Appearances counted for a lot in our middle-class household. You did not say what you thought, you said what was acceptable – and did what was appropriate. At least that's how I got by until faced with an alternative.
>
> In looking back, what I wanted more than anything was to feel loved for who I was, not conditionally based on my acceptable behavior. All this is prelude to saying that at the age of sixteen I entered into a sexual relationship with our parish minister. I knew it was wrong and yet for all my acculturation in what was acceptable – I selfishly chose the excitement of being desired (mistaking it for love) over remaining an average teen. Thirty years later, I am still paying the consequences of that choice. At the time it felt exhilarating for a "good" girl to be living an evil adult life. Although I started out naïve, I soon became jaded and hardened to the reality of my double life. After three years of lies and selfish gratification it all fizzled out.

The relief of not having to manipulate, connive, and conspire was incredible. A few months later I met the man who would become my husband. It was thrilling to have a relationship with someone my own age rather than with a married man fifteen years my senior. I can remember feeling clean, open, and honest for the first time in many years. And yet I know now I wasn't. Our marriage could have worked if we'd had the self-discipline to take the time to grow trust and openness rather than share a bed.

Our relationship began to fall apart even before we were married. My husband couldn't bear the knowledge of my previous relationship – nor did he ever feel his parents approved of our marriage. Theirs was another family where only acceptable behavior was appropriate. Our marriage was a hard, lonely, and disappointing eight-month-long slog. We were two selfish brats who made half-hearted attempts to please one another. I ended up leaving to "think things over."

I was gone long enough to get a job and ended up working with a man I'll call Frank, who would again change my life. I was carrying around a lot of conflicting emotions in those days – I had been ever since it all started five years earlier – but what

I remember most was my overwhelming sense of failure – this time it was *my* marriage that had failed and I had no clue of what to do to make it work. I was backed into a corner and could not lie or cheat my way out. I remember feeling a deep hunger to find something by which to guide my life – I described it as a truth that would not change.

That's when Frank began to talk to me about right and wrong, life and death, obedience and sin. I thought I was too cool for religion but something in me listened. And after a while it even began to make sense.

But talk was just talk – about six months later I experienced something very real. I was working alone in the photo darkroom (a great place to think) and remember standing there and being overwhelmed with all the deceitful, selfish and evil things I had done in my short life. One by one I saw the faces of the people whose lives I had ruined, actually trampled over, in my drive for selfish gratification.

It was frightening – but even more frightening was the realization that I was not able to redeem myself. I had tried before I met my husband, and yet here I was two years later having left even more trampled people in my wake. What was it going to take to change me? I did *not* want to have a rerun of this revelation on my deathbed with fifty more years of broken relationships added on top.

Until that moment I couldn't have said I believed in God – but in my desperation I begged God to help me, admitting I couldn't help myself. That was the first time in my life I chose what was right over what was exciting. I remember the two alternatives: continue as I had been, calling my own shots and deal with the consequences, or choose to believe and change.

Belief certainly appeared to be the less glamorous of the two choices. But the change I felt was instantaneous. I walked out of that darkroom with new eyes, new ears and a new heart. Nothing looked the same as it had before. I was given a chance to totally start over and life was once again worth living. I still find it incredible and look on it as a touchstone for other experiences that came later...

Grace says that though she knew this change to be "total and absolute," Frank, who had meanwhile become her partner in a new business they co-founded, was unable to believe in it. (Strangely, many of us seem incapable of believing that others – even people we know well – are capable of change. We ourselves feel certain that we have grown wiser, humbler, or holier with time, and yet we often judge even those we claim to love most by things they said or did years ago.)

To make a long story short, what started as a wonderful conversion experience became another hell. Having delivered me from living a lie, Frank now sought to control every aspect of my life. At first, being a young convert, I accepted his hovering; slowly, however, I began to realize it was a perverse preoccupation. It was a cruel game, but whenever I tried to challenge it, he tried to blackmail me with my former life.

Frank had a violent temper: along with the members of his nice "Christian" family, I found myself facing his fists more than once. His need to control also took the form of attempted rape. Having been there before, I knew I couldn't carry that kind of guilt again and managed to avert disaster. But I was still living a lie. And this time it was much harder to expose, because that would mean giving up my partnership in our very lucrative business, and relinquishing my wealth and the lifestyle that came with it.

It was only when I stopped running in place long enough that I could admit I was depressed and unhappy. I longed to rediscover the freeing that had come with my first experience of belief, and I promised God I would give him everything I had to regain a close relationship with Him...

An additional angle to repentance is the way it draws people together. On the surface this may seem unlikely: after all, repentance means self-exposure – an act we associate with the privacy of the psychiatrist's office or confessional, and with the guarantee of confidentiality. But as M. Scott Peck points out in his book *A Different Drum,* that's only one part of the equation. Everyone, he writes, has something to expose. Every human being is in some way vulnerable and incomplete. And so, instead of letting our brokenness divide us, as it so often does, we ought to recognize it as the unifying quality it is, and see it as a reason for community:

> How strange that we should ordinarily feel compelled to hide our wounds when we are all wounded! Community requires the ability to expose our wounds and weaknesses to our fellow

creatures. It also requires the ability to be affected by the wounds of others... But even more important is the love that arises among us when we share, both ways, our woundedness.

Grace found this love, once she emerged from the painful crucible of self-examination:

> In the end, the renewal I was looking for cost everything. I had to take action and resign from the business I'd helped to build. I sold my vacation home, and after that the townhouse in the city where I worked. I dropped my career. My whole life took a new turn as I tried to discern what *God* wanted me to do...But in doing all this, I was amazed, once again, at how quickly the deepest yearnings of my heart were filled. I felt like I was given a clean slate to start life completely over. Beyond that, the experience led me – further than I had ever been led before – out of myself, and to community with others.

Given the fickleness of human nature, the proverbial clean slate is an impermanent thing, and the same goes for love and community. Though perfect in the abstract, in real life they weather quickly and, like once-shiny medallions, must be refurbished again

and again. This is why I am so certain that true rebirth has nothing to do with "eternal life insurance."
Yes, death brings new life. But what then? Are we to
remain content in the state of a newborn, unable to
crawl, stand, or walk? Or is there something more
required of us?

Ann Morrow Lindbergh, a woman who suffered
repeatedly during her life, suggests there is. She says
our task as human beings is not merely to be reborn,
but also to *grow*, and to do that, she says, we cannot
only die, but must remain continually vulnerable –
"open to love, though also hideously open to the
possibility of more suffering."

For the person who fears change, that may seem
an unwelcome thought. But for anyone who has experienced it, it is a veritable lifeline. To quote Grace
one more time:

> My first conversion, if you want to call it that, was
> a life-changing thing. So were my subsequent new
> beginnings. But life doesn't stop. And I've come to
> realize that if I am going to live it authentically, I
> must continually go through new cycles of repen-
> tance and renewal. I look forward to those times
> because that's when I'm most alive.

travel guides

Precisely because I do not have
the beautiful words I need, I call
upon my acts to speak to you.

DAISY ZAMORA

Rebirth is wonderful, but if we do not nourish the new life it implies, it will quickly weaken and die. And this is especially true when our transformation is only partial. I've seen time and again how one little thing – a petty but cherished grudge, a secret sin – can wreck a marriage, a church, or a life. Therefore it's crucial, whenever we feel changes occurring within us, to be open to every insight that they bring. We will have to make hard decisions, but this won't be a grim duty. If the heaven within us is real, it will spill out from us and ripple into the world around us, not as a form of personal power, but as a life-giving rivulet that can quench any thirst.

That's a far cry from the popular sort of rebirth offered by the two biggest spiritual industries of our day – the New Age movement and "born again" Christianity – that often deliver far less than they promise. They begin and end with no more than the enlightenment or salvation of the isolated individual. The selfishness of these movements, which is cousin to the cult of greed enshrined in our economic system, may drive up the widespread popularity they enjoy. But in the end such egocentric teachings don't work. You can't have a purely private heaven.

Insects, plants, animals, and microbes survive only because of community, the individual depending on the whole. It's exactly the same with us. As Martin Luther King remarked, "It really boils down to this: that all life is interrelated. We are all...tied into a single garment of destiny." The battle between heaven and hell begins in our own hearts, but it encompasses everything: economics, culture, religion, politics. Our personal rebirth joins us to the rebirth of the world. It's here that we'll find the reason and mission for our life. This should fill us with wonder and awe. What a mistake if at this very point we lose courage and try to evade the demands of transformation! That would be a form of spiritual suicide.

While writing this book I've often thought back to three people who have stretched me to understand life's battles in a fuller, more fundamental way. To me, their stories are worth reflecting on because they illustrate several basic themes. Not that we should hold them up as heroes, or attempt to emulate them – as the first-generation Quakers of York advised their descendants, every new generation must find its own way: "We do not want you to copy or imitate us. We want to be like a ship that has crossed the ocean, leaving a wake of foam, which soon fades away. We want you to follow the spirit, which we have sought to follow." Still, in looking to those who have gone before us, I am certain that each of us can gain confidence to travel the path that we ourselves feel we must walk.

CHE GUEVARA

Years ago, I wouldn't have picked Che Guevara as an example of someone whose life gives hands and feet to rebirth. Far from an inspiring figure, he struck me as a misguided genius. Long a popular icon of radicals and advertisers, he was also, to my mind, a cold-blooded man of violence, and I found nothing attractive in his philosophy of life. After all, I've always believed that peace can only be achieved by non-violent means, whereas Che is hardly known for pacifist tendencies. As an internationally-known guerrilla, he was instrumental not only in bringing revolution to Cuba, but in organizing armed struggles in the Congo and Bolivia as well.

My prejudices dissolved after visiting Cuba and discovering that this man – though murdered over thirty years ago – still lives on in the hearts of a new generation. I met Che's spirit in one of the last places I would have expected it: at a Baptist church in Havana. I was speaking to a youth group about non-violence and forgiveness, and the ongoing struggle for civil rights in the United States (the church is named after Martin Luther King), and when I asked them if there was anyone they looked up to as a fighter for social change, they immediately responded by telling me about Che and what he meant to them. The sparkle in their eyes was unforgettable.

It's been said that a bad tree cannot bear good fruit. As I learned more about Che's life, I came to see his vision and his deeds as a sharp and much-deserved rebuke to Christians who claim to have left everything to serve their fellow human beings. Trained as a physician from an upper-middle-class Argentinean family, he abandoned his considerable opportunities for a greater cause. He traveled up and down Latin America and saw firsthand how the common people were ground down by a ruthless land-owning class supported by American business and military interests. He joined Fidel Castro's rebel group determined to overthrow the corrupt and murderous dictatorship in Cuba, and his leadership qualities became clear in combat.

Promoted to the rank of commander, he nevertheless accepted no concessions for himself, at great personal cost to his physical health. Severely asthmatic, often without the medications he needed and desperate for air, he still lugged his own bags and weapons through the mountains, jungles, and swamps. (Che's good-humored disregard for his health was well known. When his doctor limited him to one cigar a day, he went to the manufacturer and ordered custom-made Havanas that were twice the normal size.)

After Castro's triumph over the Batista regime in 1959, Che threw himself into the formidable task of reorganizing Cuban society. His high idealism was legendary, but even more remarkable was the absence of any drive for personal political power. His demands on himself were relentless. After six days of working eighteen-hour days at his government job during the week, he'd volunteer his Sunday mornings to help with the sugar cane harvest or work as a stevedore. His dedication to fighting for the poor led him to abandon his position of power in Havana to join freedom fighters first in Africa and then in Bolivia. The words he wrote around that time, as he departed for the unknown in pursuit of his calling, still resonate today:

Let me say, with the risk of appearing ridiculous, that the true revolutionary is guided by strong feelings of love. It is impossible to think of an authentic revolutionary without this quality... One must have a large dose of humanity, a large dose of a sense of justice and truth, to avoid falling into extremes, into cold intellectualism, into isolation from the masses. Every day we must struggle so that this love of living humanity is transformed into concrete facts, into acts that will serve as an example...

To quote him further, from his last letter to his children:

Above all, try always to feel deeply any injustice committed against any person in any part of the world. It is the most beautiful quality of a revolutionary.

It was this vision of love and transformation – and Che's willingness to give his life in order to make it reality – that inspired these young people. As they spoke about what he'd taught them about self-sacrifice in service to the causes of economic and social justice, the words of President Kennedy (ironically, Che's implacable enemy) came to my mind: "Ask not what your country can do for you, but what you can do for your country."

Che's last mission to Bolivia in 1967 proved unsuccessful. When the Bolivian army unit hunting down his doomed band of guerrillas captured him in the jungle, he was a defeated man, physically worn down and despondent over the deaths of his comrades. A CIA operative working with the army unit informed him that he was to be shot, and later reported to Washington:

> Early in the morning, the unit receives the order to execute Guevara and the other prisoners. When Sgt. Terán (the executioner) enters the room, Guevara stands up with his hands tied and states, "I know what you have come for. I am ready."
>
> Terán tells him to be seated and leaves the room for a few moments. When Terán comes back, Guevara stands up and refuses to be seated. Finally, Guevara tells him: "Know this now, you are killing a man." These are his last words. Terán fires his M2 carbine and kills him.

Jesus taught that not all those who say, "Lord, Lord" will enter heaven. The prize, he said, is for the man who loves his sisters and brothers so deeply that he will lay down his life for them. Che did exactly that. His failures aside – he could be ruthless to enemies and traitors – he laid down his life for the suffering people with whom he identified, not just in dying but all along the way. His example would go on to inspire many, from the European student demonstrators of 1968, to Nelson Mandela in the 1980s, to the Zapatista rebels of Mexico today.

Che showed that when we have found a vision to live by, no sacrifice will be too great for us, not even our physical death – which explains the French philosopher Jean-Paul Sartre's remark that Che was "the most complete human being of our age." I have come to believe that he wasn't just a great revolutionary, but also, despite his shortcomings and his sins, a better follower of Christ than most who claim that label.

What exactly was the heart of Che's vision, that it still animates young people around the world? His words on the revolutionary power of love hint at one answer. So, perhaps, does a poem found in his backpack after his death:

Christ, I love you,
not because you descended from a star,
but because you revealed to me
man's tears and anguish;
showed me the keys that open
the closed doors of light.
Yes, you taught me that man is God,
a poor God crucified like you.
The one at your left,
at Golgotha – the worst thief –
he, too, is God.

Leon Felipe

DOROTHY DAY

How should we live when we realize that God is present in everyone we meet? "The mystery of the poor is this," said Dorothy Day, "that they are Jesus, and whatever you do for them you do to him." Founder of the Catholic Worker (a loosely organized movement of urban hospitality houses for the unemployed and homeless), Dorothy's vision penetrated the off-putting external appearances of the many "worst thieves" she served, and saw divinity:

"Those who cannot see the face of Christ in the poor are atheists indeed."

Her life was accordingly a radical one, and her friendship influenced me deeply from the first day I met her in the mid-1950s, until her death in 1980. When she passed away in the cramped Lower East Side room she called home, hundreds of thousands mourned her. Archbishops compared her to Gandhi and Martin Luther King, *The New York Times* spoke of the "end of an era," wealthy admirers organized a memorial mass, and unemployed men wept. Who was this old woman?

Born in Brooklyn in 1897, Dorothy's early years were marked by dramatic twists and turns – journalism school in Illinois, travel in Europe, and writing jobs in Hollywood and New York. It was a whirlwind youth, and left her reeling from a broken marriage, an abortion, and a series of unhappy relationships.

In 1926 Dorothy had a baby, Tamar – an event that changed her, or at least cemented an earlier yearning for a more wholesome, fruitful life. Long attracted to Catholicism (despite her bohemian excesses), she turned to the Gospels, and found in them the beginnings of a faith. Soon she experienced a deep-going conversion.

Friends and acquaintances laughed at her "religion," but Dorothy was not to be deterred. While admitting that the Christianity she knew was far from perfect, she argued that the just society they were all looking for must be built on God. Not that she was content with conventional church life. Having grown up on Dickens and Sinclair, she identified with the working class and sought, in her own words, a faith that would "not just minister to slaves, but...do away with slavery." And so she threw herself into what she called the "works of mercy," feeding and housing the homeless, writing and speaking out against the evil of war, demonstrating on behalf of migrant workers and marching against the death penalty.

Articulate and outspoken, she upset people of every ideological camp. The Vatican felt she was too cozy with Communism; the secular press was embarrassed by her faith. Conservatives chafed every time she went to jail for civil disobedience; left-leaning

friends applauded her subversiveness but found her
ideas on morality far too straight-laced and "tradi-
tional." Dorothy's concern was never politics as such,
however. It was the love of God, which she claimed is
meaningless unless it finds expression in love to one's
neighbor.

> It is not love in the abstract that counts. Men have
> loved a cause as they have loved a woman. They
> have loved the brotherhood, the workers, the
> poor, the oppressed – but they have not loved
> man; they have not loved the least of these. They
> have not loved "personally." It is hard to love. It is
> the hardest thing in the world, naturally speaking.
> Have you ever read Tolstoy's *Resurrection?* He
> tells of political prisoners in a long prison train,
> enduring chains and persecution for the love of
> their brothers, ignoring those same brothers on
> the long trek to Siberia. It is never the brothers
> right next to us, but the brothers in the abstract
> that are easy to love.

Dorothy's words remind us that while it is tempting
to try to change the world in sweeping ways, our actions all too often fall short of our ideals. And thus
she reminded her co-workers that it is the person

next to us whose needs we can best attend to, and
whose hurts we ought to heal first. She not only
spoke of this invisible or "little" way, but devoted
herself to it tirelessly, year after year.

During the Great Depression, Dorothy spent her
days serving bread and coffee to homeless men.
When New York's next recession came, in the early
1970s, she was still doing the same thing. A cynic
might have trouble with this; Dorothy did not. To
her, even the most modest attempt to solve poverty
was valid, because it was better than doing nothing:

> What we would like to do is change the world –
> make it a little simpler for people to feed, clothe,
> and shelter themselves as God intended for them
> to do. And, by fighting for better conditions, by
> crying out unceasingly for the rights of the work-
> ers, of the poor, of the destitute... we can work for
> the oasis, the little cell of joy and peace in a harried
> world. We can throw our pebble in the pond and
> be confident that its ever-widening circle will
> reach around the world.

HEINRICH ARNOLD

Though the stories of larger-than-life figures are inspiring, they are often met with sighs: in comparison with our own lives, they seem like impossible acts to follow. Fortunately, we all know someone – a mentor, grandparent, favorite relative or former teacher – whose day-to-day example means more to us than the deeds of the great and famous. In my case, that person was my father.

Like me, my father, Heinrich Arnold, worked on and off as a pastor. When I was a boy, our family lived in an isolated community of European war refugees in the backwoods of Paraguay. Though my father never studied at seminary – he was an agronomist by training – he was a natural *Seelsorger,* the German term for someone who "cares for souls." Even when he was only fifteen, adults spontaneously confided in him and asked him for advice.

It was not as if my father were an openly religious man. He rarely if ever preached, and was, generally speaking, a man of few words. For him, faith was not something to be talked about, but something to be lived. Loving God meant loving the poor, and because he grew up in a household whose open door welcomed a constant stream of tramps, union organizers, and radicals, he identified with them from early childhood on.

When we lived in South America, he occasionally hired men from the nearest village to help bring in the harvest or do other work on the farm. One day one of them sneaked into our apartment to steal bed sheets and other household items. Luckily the dog raised the alarm and chased the man outdoors, where he narrowly escaped being bitten by scrambling up the nearest tree. Running out of the house to see what all the noise was, my father called off the dog, reassured the man that he was unarmed, and invited him into the house. There he offered him a meal, and found out why the man had tried to rob us: he was the sole breadwinner of his large family, and he was not making ends meet.

Later, when we moved to New York, he connected just as easily with more sophisticated people, including the educated seekers that flocked to our new home. Here, as in South America (and before that, England, and Germany), people came to him without any overtures or persuasion on his part. Once or twice complete strangers turned to him on a plane or train and unburdened themselves to him. Pondering the reason for such signs of trust, I've come to feel that a big part of it was my father's deep love for every soul he encountered. On meeting him, people instinctively felt this love, and it disarmed them. Part of it was also his belief that despite their varied exteriors, every human being is fundamentally the same, which led him to treat every person with the same respect. I'll never forget him telling me, after returning from a stay in the hospital, that that is the place you really see how similar people are.

In a hospital, men and women of every income bracket and social background come to be treated. When they come in, they look very different: some are awkward and dressed in filthy clothes, others are meticulously groomed and have expensive suits. But then the nurse takes them out to get ready for surgery, and when they return, half-naked and half-gowned, they all look the same – though some are potbellied. Yes, we're all unique, my father would say, but underneath, we all know the conflict between heaven and hell, and all desire rebirth.

Recently Suzanne, a long-time friend, wrote to me about the first time she met my father. A mother and Harvard dropout by the age of twenty-three, Suzanne had already abandoned her idealist phase. With a good job at a glossy magazine, she had also risen to the challenge of raising a daughter on her own. She felt she'd seen enough of the world to know that the only worthwhile goal for her was to live fast and fabulously.

Suzanne was an ardent atheist; all the same she confessed to feeling haunted by guilt over an abortion she had procured in the course of an affair. It was at this juncture, during a visit to Woodcrest, our home in upstate New York, that she met my father. (Woodcrest was the first American settlement of the Bruderhof, the Christian community movement I grew up in; my father was a pastor or "servant" in the community.)

> I visited for a couple of days, and I felt that the assumptions that had guided my life were being shaken. After lunch one day, I see a person coming toward me. Tall, thin, lurching, and in spite of all that, clearly the embodiment of goodness and love. He is approaching *me*, wretched, befouled

by every sin. What has he to do with me? My
only thought is, don't say anything, just don't say
a word. I look at the floor. I await the judgment
to come. I wait. I wait. Nothing comes. Horrors,
a tear is rolling down my cheek. At last the silence is broken. Then "goodness" speaks, "Come
with me." I follow after him, too numb to care
what happens.

We go upstairs and into a shabby little office.
Salvation Army furniture. He precedes me. He
turns around. He looks at me and says, "A cup of
coffee, you need a cup of coffee. I make you a cup
of coffee." And the huge, awkward, good man
goes through countless steps to create, in a room
singularly unprepared with the implements, a cup
of coffee. Apologizes that there is no milk and
sugar, and hands me the cup. Next Suzanne-the-
child-murderer was pouring forth words to the
coffee maker. When I ran out of hideous things to
say, Heinrich, for that was his name, said "Thank
you for the trust."

Later it seemed to me that we had lived through
the entire gospel, and the gospel was, as I had always suspected way down deep inside me, "C'mon
in, sit down, have a cup of coffee." It had nothing to
do with sitting in wooden pews. It had to do with
goodness's compassionate love for badness.

At the end, I told Heinrich that I would now return to New York City. Heinrich said, "That is death." I said, "I know it is death." But I was thinking, I know all this has happened, but I'll just go back and pick up living again as if nothing had happened.

But some things could not so easily be reversed. I, who had in my despair been spending too much money in fashionable restaurants at lunch hour, found my feet taking me to the greasy spoons of Second and Third Avenues. The food was ambrosia, the people were "us." I now knew I belonged with the poor, forever. What had happened to me? My taste buds had changed, my eyes were different, my ears, my nose, my sense of touch…I was Suzanne poured into a differently perceiving vessel.

I spent three months as "the different person" trying to escape God, who, I knew, would require the death of my "old self." Oh, how the devil tried to lure me! (And how I tried to follow him.) He offered me money and fame in the strangest ways. But I could not eat the foul dish he set before me. I turned from it in disgust. I had nowhere to go but back to the community.

I went back with my three-year-old daughter, Judy, who had loved every minute of our first visit. I was shaking like a leaf, wondering what kind of a religious nut I was becoming. On the door of our room was a sign scrawled by a child, "Welcome Home Judy and Suzanne." My personal boulder rolled away. I was home – home at last! Why had I stayed away so long?

After this I was as one in love. I was utterly consumed by the concerns of the fellowship I'd become a part of. The struggles of all the members, so openly shared, seemed to be my struggle. It was more like an ongoing adventure in discovering God's will. Punctuated by laughter, of all things! This adventure had nothing in common with a gloomy, introspective, mining operation. Life was unutterably beautiful, wonderful. All I had been through – and now, living each day was forgiveness, was prayer, was God. That a wretch like me was allowed *this*.

The price would be paid, however. This life in community was a pearl. It cost me something: my estranged husband, who had been the one to convince me to come to the community in the first place, decided it wasn't for him after several months. A while later, I got the divorce papers in the mail.

Suzanne remained friends with my parents for the next thirty-five years – that is, until they died. She now says she credits that simple experience of coffee and a conversation with my father – his mundane act of compassion and understanding – with being a catalyst for her rebirth.

Perhaps my father could communicate so much to people like Suzanne while saying so little because he *felt* so strongly; a passionate man, he did not always need words to express himself. Perhaps it was his refusal to cultivate the personal charisma so often admired in spiritual leaders, or his insistence that a pastor's task is to lead his congregation to God, not to himself. Perhaps it was the agonies he himself went through that made him sensitive to the burdens that others carried and allowed him to see straight into their souls, so to speak. Whatever the case, people trusted him, and as their trust grew, it gained him the enmity of jealous colleagues.

This was especially so during my parents' first years in Paraguay. True, most members of their community had escaped the bombing terrors of wartime England unharmed, but at what cost? Now they were miles from nowhere, in the middle of an unfriendly South American jungle – slaves to the unrelenting sun and to insects, malnourishment, and disease. Children died, including my baby sister.

Sadly, far from uniting the community, these hardships embittered many. Over time, these members lost their original fire and – callous, confused, and blinded by their grief – looked to the ablest, most efficient men in the community for quick answers. Meanwhile my father, who felt that the real solution was compassion (not better organization), spoke out against the increasing regimentation of the group. Arguing that it was more important to attend to the needs of those who were sick, weak, mentally ill, or otherwise marginalized, he appealed to any who would listen to soften their hearts – to rediscover God and their own humanity.

One who did not appreciate such talk was the settlement's doctor, who accidentally overmedicated my father during a serious illness in 1941 with the primitive bromides then used for sedation. Though sobered by the hallucinations and mood swings that my father suffered as a result, his doctor never owned up to their real cause – bad enough – but instead suggested that they were symptomatic of "obsessional neurosis." On the basis of this spurious diagnosis, my father was removed from his job as pastor. Worse, he was robbed of his confidence and plagued – for the next twenty-six years – by the thought that perhaps he was indeed mentally unstable. (It was only in 1968 that a new family doctor, reviewing his records, discovered the cover-up and brought it to light.)

Two years later, when my father again protested the callous and spiritually brutal leadership in the isolated community, he was expelled with only the equivalent of a day's wages, separated from his pregnant wife and four children. Knowing only a little Spanish, he felt like a fish out of water; worse, when he turned to fellow German immigrants, he discovered that most were pro-Nazi, and had little sympathy for people like him, who had fled the old country as a member of a "seditious group." The only work he could find was in a leper colony, living constantly under the fear that he might contract leprosy, which was then believed to be contagious. According to the practice of the time, infection with leprosy would have meant permanent separation from his family and friends.

The twenty months during which my father was torn from our family were hard for him and for us, but his return, which might have been joyous, was strained. Showing him their youngest daughter, who'd been born in his absence, my mother expected him to share her joy. But the hardships of the last two years had numbed him, and he was unable to respond to her happiness. Not surprisingly, she read this uncharacteristic lack of warmth as coldness.

In the long run, however, this dark chapter did not embitter my father. Instead, it left him determined to prevent human cruelty whenever he could, and increased his already unusual capacity to forgive. As children, for instance, we had no idea of what my parents had suffered: they resisted self-pity, and never said anything derogatory or negative about anyone – not even the doctor who had led him to believe he was unstable. Only years later, when I was married, did I find out what they had gone through in the past.

My father's suffering also left him with a life-long empathy for others in need. Even after psychiatrists advised my father that there was no point in "wasting more time" on this or that troubled individual, he would reach out again and again, calling, visiting, and writing. Through his persistence, I saw many "hopeless cases" find a renewed purpose for living. One person I particularly remember was Nick, a homeless alcoholic, drug addict, and Navy vet whom he counseled in the mid-1970s. (Tragically, Nick ultimately succumbed to despair: after making progress under my father's care, he moved to another state, went rapidly downhill, and killed himself. When my father heard the news, he wept as if he had lost his own son.)

Needless to say, my father made mistakes as a man and pastor, as he was the first to acknowledge. He could misjudge situations, and he was not above losing his temper at times. From my point of view as his son, however, his most obvious "weakness" was the endless tenderness he showed not only to family members, friends, and colleagues, but also to strangers and even to people who betrayed him. No matter how deeply they had hurt him, he would battle through his feelings until he was able to trust again – even if objectively speaking, all grounds for trust were gone. When I grew frustrated over his willingness to be hurt a second time, he would tell me, "I'd much rather trust and be betrayed, than live in mistrust for a single day." He proved this declaration in deeds.

Given my father's uncanny ability to discern a person's strengths and weaknesses, many sought his advice in resolving the most intimate questions. Often he just listened quietly; other times he sought to prompt an inner recognition of what needed to be done. He was always unstintingly honest. This reassured some, but it unnerved others. His writing had a similar effect. As Catholic author Henri Nouwen said of his book *Discipleship:*

> Arnold's words touched me as a double-edged sword, calling me to choose between truth and lies, salvation and sin, selflessness and selfishness, light and darkness, God and demon. At first I wasn't sure if I wanted to be confronted in such a direct way, and I discovered some resistance in myself.

Not surprisingly, while most people my father counseled ended up being grateful, others lashed out at him. A few felt so threatened by him that they wanted to kill him: to my knowledge, at least two serious attempts were made on his life. Such hatred shook him, but it never succeeded in silencing him. To quote Nouwen a second time:

> Arnold reminds us that the peace of the Gospel is not the same as the peace of the world, that the consolation of the Gospel is not the same as the consolation of the world, and that the gentleness of the Gospel has little to do with the "free for all" attitude of the world…The Gospel asks for a choice, a radical choice, a choice that is not always praised, supported or appreciated.

My father was never influential or prominent by worldly standards. But I have seen his legacy surface in the most unexpected places. Why shouldn't it be the same for each of us? Why don't we dare to believe that the fruits of our faith will blossom in ways we never see, out of proportion to the small seeds we plant? And isn't the hope of the sower a small piece of heaven?

angels

If the angel deigns to come, it will be
because you have convinced him –
and not by your tears, but by your
resolve to make a beginning.

RAINER MARIA RILKE

For people who argue that human life
ends with physical death, the transformation of a
butterfly may seem an irrelevant, if interesting, image. But for us who believe in eternity, it is a sign of
the hope we have in another life that is even greater
than the rebirth brought about by repentance. It reminds us of the resurrection of the dead whereby
we will (to quote the New Testament) be "raised

incorruptible." This rebirth will be granted "to those who believe," we are told, and it will be preceded by a day of judgment on which they will be separated from those who do not.

For centuries, philosophers and theologians have argued over the nature and meaning of that judgment, and about the existence of heaven and hell. Writers, poets, and painters have grappled with the subject too. There is André Gide, who said that "just like the kingdom of God, hell is within us"; Dante, with his vivid scenes of purgatory; and Brueghel, with his graphic depictions of terrible monsters and dismembered bodies. There's also Dostoevsky, whose character Father Zossima shuns the idea of such physical torments and says that hell is rather the suffering of being unable to love:

> People talk of hellfire in the material sense. I don't go into that mystery...But if there were a literal fire, I imagine those in hell would be glad of it, for in material agony, their still greater spiritual agony would be forgotten for a moment.

Those who incline toward more literal interpretations of the Bible may grate at this view of hell, indeed, they may shoot holes in it. What about the reference to the place where there will be weeping and gnashing of teeth? What about the pit of Sheol and the everlasting lake of fire? In answer to similar questions, Mumia Abu-Jamal, a friend and writer, says:

> Whole religions have based their appeal on such visions, and in turn used fear to build their earthly mansions and cathedrals. There may well be a hell that is an underworld. But who among us will dare deny that hell has been – and is – an unquestionable reality right here on earth?
>
> The history of Africa and the Americas, while glorious from the European point of view, can only be seen as having been hellish for the so-called natives. Their history is one of massacres, genocides, and holocausts. And to the present-day remainders of these nations' indigenous peoples, their life of abject poverty, rule and ridicule by the arrogant descendants of the invaders, must seem hellish indeed.
>
> Speaking of holocausts, one cannot ignore the suffering of millions of Jews, Poles, Romani, and others under Hitler during the dark years of his Third Reich, and other mass-killings since then. As Christopher Marlowe put it in *Doctor Faustus:*

Hell hath no limits nor is circumscribed
In one self place; for where we are is Hell,
And to be short, when all the world dissolves,
And every creature shall be purified,
All places shall be hell, that are not heaven.

When a child in poverty dies of starvation, there is hell. When people groan under the boot of oppression, there is hell. Where there is any injustice, there is hell. Doesn't this sound like an apt description of far too much of the human condition?

As for heaven, there are just as many points of view. The Bible itself contains no single clear picture. In some verses we are told that it will be nigh impossible for the rich to enter heaven; in others, that there are mansions there waiting for children and the childlike. Still other passages imply salvation for everyone, and include the promise that *every* tear will be dried, and that God will reconcile all things in the universe to himself. Then there is the saying, "The kingdom of heaven is within you," which seems simple enough to comprehend. Heaven must be elsewhere too, however, for it is said that the angels descended from it to announce Jesus' birth, and that he later returned to it on a cloud.

Surely, hell and heaven are more than subjective
states of mind – more than handy metaphors for anger and love, discord and harmony, pleasure and
pain. If they weren't, how to explain the self-hatred
that drives a depressive person toward suicide, or the
peace that washes over someone who, after years of
holding grudges, has suddenly been able to forgive?
How to explain the fact that we can feel far away
from a living person right next to us, but intimately
bound to a deceased family member or friend? How
is it that the limitations imposed by physical circumstances may yield, at times, to an atmosphere that is
wholly independent of them – that it is possible to
feel the weight of oppression in a house of worship,
but hope and joy in a prison cell on death row? Are
such powers merely internal emotions, or do they
reflect greater forces that originate in another sphere
or plane? To me, the answer is self-evident: both
heaven and hell exist as realities in and of themselves.

This assertion is a matter of belief, of course, and
cannot be proved. Yet throughout history, windows
have been opened here and there, allowing believers
and unbelievers alike glimpses into greater realities,

inspiring or terrifying them, but always leaving them
with the unshakable belief that there are other
worlds. Literature abounds on the experiences of
people who have talked to, seen, or felt the presence of
tormented departed souls. So do accounts of people
who have seen or heard angels, often at the hour of a
loved one's death.

For most of us, however, it is the hells and heavens
of the human heart that we must contend with, because that is where we experience their force. Few
people are granted more than an inkling of the vast
worlds that exist beyond our own, and in my experience, they tend to be reticent, reverent, and filled
with awe.

That is one reason I have not focused on these
things in this book. Another is my discomfort with
the curiosity that leads to the sensationalization of
demons and angels and the like. Besides, I believe
that since God set us into a material world, we ought
to live in it fully – in the here and now. Even if our
present life is meant to be a preparation for a better
life to come, there is no point in frittering away our
days worrying about the future, or our chances for

eternal blessedness. Jesus taught us, "Love your
neighbor as yourself," and that simple command
holds more than a life's work.

The following words of Blumhardt, written in response to a theologian who asked him for his views
on heaven and hell, amplify my point:

> People think that after they die everything will
> suddenly fall into place. But if you do not have
> eternal life here, do you really think it will be any
> better over there? What gives you that hope? It
> would seem to me that when people die they will
> be just the same afterward as before. If they see
> and hear nothing but themselves in this life,
> won't it be the same for them in the next? But if
> they are gripped by eternity while still on earth,
> then dying – the laying aside of the body – will
> pale in comparison to beginning a new life full of
> heavenly joys.

A passage from C. S. Lewis's *Mere Christianity*
makes much the same point, even more forcefully
and clearly:

> When the Author walks onto the stage the play is
> over. And what is the good of saying you are on His
> side then, when you see the whole natural universe

melting away like a dream and something else comes crashing in...something so beautiful to some and so terrible to others that none of us will have any choice left? This time God will be so overwhelming that he will strike either irresistible love or irresistible horror into every creature. It will be too late then to choose your side...That will be the time when we discover which side we have really chosen. Now, today...is our chance to choose.

To be gripped by eternity while still in the clutch of time; to live for heaven in a world that often seems more like hell; to live for love and humility in a culture that rewards selfishness, greed, and self-aggrandizement – this clearly demands a daily fight. It may be a spiritual one, but that does not make it any less real; for the irreconcilable forces of life and death often clash in painful, concrete ways. That truth is illustrated well enough by the stories in this book, but it was driven home for me by Carole, a close friend who died of cancer in 1998. I'll quote her directly, from an interview she gave a few months before her death:

> When I found out that I had cancer, I felt somehow relieved – I don't know why. Maybe it's because I had always been afraid of dying, and all of a

sudden there it was, and I didn't have to worry about it anymore. Sure, I've gone to pieces over it since then. After the first bout of chemo, I felt this lump under my arm, and I just fell apart.

On the other hand, I've been almost frantically afraid of cancer all my life, but then when it came, right there, square in my face, I wasn't afraid...My husband, Dale, even joked that it would be a terrible shame if I died of something else, since I had worried so much about cancer all my life.

Still, you can't just lie down and accept it, because it's a deadly disease. You can't just fold up and crash. You have to fight with everything you have. That's why I went for chemotherapy. I felt it was the answer, because with chemo you're really fighting the disease with everything you have. I was going to take the most explosive kind, you know – whatever it took.

Then I found out that the survival rate for my type of cancer was basically nil, one to ninety-nine. But I hadn't asked, and I didn't care. I already knew from my sister's death [of the same disease] that the statistics were pretty bleak. So I said, "Forget the numbers. I'm not going to spend the rest of my life in bed, sick and vomiting and everything else. I'm going to live with everything I've got."

What does it mean to fight for your life? Well, Dale and I start each day by reading the Gospels, and it absolutely blows my mind every time I read those words. Jesus did and said just what he felt, straight out. He loved everyone without reservation – the rich and the poor. And at the same time he tackled people when they sinned: with compassion, but straightforwardly. Not that I could ever do that. But that's how I've wanted to live my life, with that kind of fervor.

You know, we spend so much of our time dealing with petty problems and thinking petty thoughts, and I've come to see that that just has to go. We hurt one another, and get hurt over little things. But it's stupid – just plain stupid – to spend time on those things.

With cancer you begin to realize that you have to make use of every day; each minute becomes precious. Dale and I have talked about how we've probably wasted years of our lives carrying little grudges and things that we couldn't work out, or struggling to find enough humility to confront a problem, or apologize, or whatever. So you're going to think this is weird, but to me having cancer has been like an adventure, the adventure of my life.

The present moment – the time we have right now – is the same for you as it is for me or for anyone. It's all we have. We tend to think, "I'll do that tomorrow;" or, "I'll wait till I have time to follow through on that…" But we actually don't have tomorrow. None of us does. We only have today and we only have each other – the person next to us, the person we live with or work with. Seeing this has been a tremendous challenge to me.

I'm not saying we all have to be intense or energetic. But each of us has a life to live – and once we've found it, we ought to live for it. We need to be ready to give up everything else that distracts us from that – our plans, absolutely everything, in order to go after what we've found. To really live demands all your fire.

Mariam, an Iraqi seven-year-old my wife and I got to know last fall, is another cancer sufferer with an equally impressive outlook on life. Unlike Carole, Mariam may not be conscious that she is engaged in a battle between life and death, and yet her fight is just as real as Carole's.

Born to poor farming parents, Mariam is one of hundreds of thousands of children in Iraq who suffer from cancer. Carpet-bombed by the USA and Britain during the short but deadly 1991 Gulf War, whole areas of the country were poisoned by the de-

pleted uranium released from the spent shells, and in
the last ten years, as leukemia, neuroblastoma, and
lymphoma rates skyrocket, more and more children
are suffering the most agonizing deaths.

As members of an international delegation bringing aid to the Middle East, my wife and I were visiting a hospital in Amman, Jordan, when we first met
Mariam. Unable to be helped in the rubble of what
was once Baghdad, this spunky little girl had been
flown out of the country by a British sponsor in order to receive the best treatment possible; but when
she finally received it, she went into a coma. She
emerged, one day before we met her, to find that
chemo had left her completely blind. Touched by
this heartbreaking development, a fellow delegate
and friend of mine from Pennsylvania arranged to
bring her to the United States.

During the next six months, Mariam showed such
resilience and cheerfulness that visitors often forgot
that she was blind and deathly ill – and on top of
that, thousands of miles from her parents, and unable to speak more than a few words of English.
Naturally extroverted, and having learned to identify dozens of friends by the sound of their voices

and footsteps, Mariam was happiest when left without supervision in a crowd of her peers. Aside from this, she had an uncanny way of finding her way to others whose disabilities set them apart.

A few days after moving to Pennsylvania, for instance, she discovered Sam, a ninety-year-old neighbor with Alzheimer's, and after greeting him, reached out to feel his beard, ears, and eyes. Sam, mystified, asked, "What do I do now?" Mariam quickly gave him a firm hug. Several weeks later Sam died, and Mariam went to the wake. This time she didn't touch him, but as she left the room where he was lying, she whispered, "Bye bye, Sam," and waved. Not long after this her travel visa expired, and Mariam returned to Iraq. Her doctors predict she will soon die.

Statistically speaking, few of us are destined to share Carole's or Mariam's fate; by the same token (to return to my grandson, Dylan, with whom I introduced this book) only a handful of us will ever know the emotional pain of disfigurement and its related ills. Still, their lives, like that of every person whose story I have related in this book, carry a meaning that is greater than the sum of their suffering. Simply put, it is the truth that even if they are denied the worldly happiness bought by popularity, attractiveness, or personal charisma, they radiate a deeper, more lasting happiness – the happiness that comes from loving and being loved. This happiness is neither based on "quality of life" nor limited by circumstances or genetic makeup. In its light even the strongest feelings of self-hatred yield. In it, even the most wretched person can find his God-given purpose, and the deep satisfaction that comes from seeking to fulfill it.

When I held my grandson Dylan for the first time, I couldn't find words to express everything I was feeling. Later I tried to put my thoughts on paper in the form of a letter – one that sparked discussion and eventually (as I've mentioned) resulted in this book. I wrote the letter to my daughter and her husband, but as I reread it now, I realize that it wasn't just meant for them:

My dear children,

Mama and I congratulate you on the birth of your Dylan, our twenty-fourth grandchild. What a joy it was to hold him yesterday – a long-awaited moment for us.

Like all our other grandchildren, Dylan will always have a special place in our hearts and prayers.

Yesterday I felt your great joy over him, but also your pain. This joy and pain is ours, too. Yes, it was a shock to see all the black marks on his little body, and only God knows what lies ahead for this courageous young fighter.

All parents hope for healthy children. But in my lifetime I've learned that a healthy body isn't necessarily the best equipped for life. Children with medical difficulties like your Dylan's will have a rough time during their growing-up years. But later on, when he gets to be my age or older, he'll look back at his childhood and marvel at God's wisdom in placing this burden on him. He will see how it prepared him for the difficulties of adult life.

Every child is a gift from God, but I see Dylan as an extra-special gift: Through Dylan, God wants to test the two of you by asking, "Do you really love me?" You and Dylan will have many hurdles to cross in his lifetime. Still, I'm convinced that whatever Dylan might lack physically, God will make up for by supplying much better gifts – learning, compassion, humor. These are gifts that are only really gained through suffering.

Having had a hard childhood myself, I can tell you that the thing that most helped me through trying times was humor. The best thing you as parents can do for Dylan is to help him develop his sense of humor. Never stop working on that. Anyone who can face hardships with true humor will be the envy of many people.

What I'm trying to say to you, my beloved children, is that God knew exactly what he was doing when he created Dylan. Because of this, the prospects for his future shine brightly, at least in my eyes. I wish you the courage to stand by him when things get tough. Remind him that "when the going gets tough, the tough get going." And when he is old enough to understand, tell him that he has grandparents who have loved him from the start and will never stop loving and praying for him.

Wishing you God's closeness,
Your Papa and Mama

Since I wrote those words, I have become even more convinced that humor – true humor, the kind that only a free heart can know – is a unique gift from God that can give people the strength to escape from their hells. Dylan may always be disfigured. But I believe he will also learn compassion for others who are "different" – and will spend more time laughing than most. In other words, as I wrote to my daughter, I am sure that her son's condition will turn out to be a blessing from God. (It's worth remembering the prophet Isaiah's saying that the Messiah himself would be mocked for his appearance: "He had no form or comeliness…and no beauty that we should desire him. He was despised and rejected of men, a man of sorrows.")

Carole certainly could laugh. She died of cancer, but that was by no means the only battle she fought in her life. Before she was diagnosed, she struggled for years with bouts of depression so severe that they landed her in the lockdown unit of a psychiatric hospital. Ultimately, however, her blunt honesty, her humor, and her compassion for others counted for more, and when she finally died it was more of a victory than a defeat.

Then there's Mariam, whose life has – at least by conventional standards – been nothing but hell, and only stands to get worse. In a worldly sense she will never find happiness or success. Yet in having touched the lives of others with her unselfconscious joy, she has undeniably fulfilled a mission, and brought them a share of light – of heaven.

When my father was a child, his mother used to set an extra place at the dinner table every night. In Jewish homes, such a place would have been for Elijah; in my father's – though it was usually taken by a homeless passerby or some other unexpected guest – it was intended for Christ.

As a family tradition, the practice was memorable enough that even when he was an old man, my father still spoke of it; as a metaphor, it gains a deeper meaning. For isn't every person – family member, stranger, enemy, or friend – a bearer of God's image stamped with the sign of eternity and carrying a divine spark? Isn't each one a messenger for whom we ought to set a place, one we should welcome and honor and love?

To view our fellow human beings in this way is not only a lofty idea; it is the only way out of confinement and alienation. Once we meet as brothers and sisters – once we can look into each other's eyes – we will know, as the Gospel of John puts it, that the light *does* shine in the darkness, and the darkness has not overcome it.

p.s.

Fulfillment, happiness, peace, freedom, justice – it doesn't matter which words you use to describe heaven. What's essential is to start on our way there. Everyone knows loneliness, woundedness, and confusion, and as we've seen, dealing with them is often an arduous, complex process. Faced with this daunting challenge, it can even be tempting to abandon our desire for heaven and to content ourselves instead by trying to make do with the hand we've been dealt.

Such resignation eventually leads to despair. Escaping from life's hells is not a matter of willpower and moral resolutions. Real transformation has nothing to do with following a given series of steps – as if we could be reborn following a how-to manual. Far from

it: we will find the way out immediately, once we realize that today is the only day that matters.

In *The Brothers Karamazov*, Dostoevsky speaks
through a character who, as he lies dying, comforts
his mother by reminding her, "One day is enough
for a man to know all happiness." If that is really so –
that what we do today has power to justify our
whole life – then the essential thing is to stop wasting our time, and to make a choice today, between
hell and heaven. It is impossible to pitch our tent in
both camps. As Jesus said, we cannot serve two mas-
ters. Either we will love the one and hate the other,
or hate the one and love the other.

Life has a way of washing us to one side of the
stream, even when we think we're successfully navi-
gating the middle. Therefore we must take action by
choosing which side we want. It's a decision we will
need to renew, but as long as we do so, we will remain
either-or people: men and women who are neither infallible nor perfect, but who, because of our conviction, can never be faulted for indifference. Weariness
and weakness will often overtake us, but we will
not be defeated, because we know every day offers

us new liberation, new heart-to-heart encounters, and
new opportunities to love. As Walt Whitman put it in
Leaves of Grass:

> This is what you shall do: Love the earth and sun
> and the animals, despise riches, give alms to every-
> one that asks, stand up for the stupid and crazy,
> devote your income and labor to others, hate ty-
> rants, argue not concerning God...

Will we choose to love, or not? Everything else pales
beside this crucial question.

index of names

Hardcover/Softcover,
264 pages.

Seeking Peace
Notes and Conversations along the Way
Johann Christoph Arnold
Preface by Thich Nhat Hanh

For anyone sick of the spiritual soup filling so many bookstore shelves these days, *Seeking Peace* is sure to satisfy a deep hunger. Arnold offers no easy solutions, but also no unrealistic promises. He spells out what peace demands. There is a peace greater than self-fulfillment, he writes. But you won't find it if you go looking for it. It is waiting for everyone ready to sacrifice the search for individual peace, everyone ready to "die to self."

Thomas Howard, St. John's Seminary
Outstanding. The candor, simplicity, and humanity of the text, but especially of the anecdotes, should recommend it to a wide reading public.

Mairead Maguire, Nobel Peace Prize laureate
Arnold inspires each of us to seek peace within our own lives...His book gives hope that we can indeed find wholeness, happiness, and harmony.

Softcover, 176 pages.

Why Forgive?
Johann Christoph Arnold

In *Why Forgive?* the reader will meet men and women who have earned the right to talk about the importance of overcoming hurt – and about the peace of mind they have found in doing so. As in life, not every story has a happy ending – a fact Arnold refuses to skirt. The book also addresses the difficulty of forgiving oneself, the temptation to blame God, and the turmoil of those who simply cannot seem to forgive, even though they try. Why forgive? Read these stories, and then decide.

ALA Booklist
A most impressive book...So powerful that tears often impede reading.

Publishers Weekly
Reminds us that to forgive is not to excuse or to anesthetize ourselves from the pain that attends life and love, but rather to enter again into life's fray.

To order: **US: 1-800-521-8011** or **724-329-1100**
UK: 0800 018 0799 or **44(0) 1580 88 33 44**
or visit our website: **www.plough.com**

Softcover, 240 pages.

Cries from the Heart
Stories of Struggle and Hope
Johann Christoph Arnold
Foreword by Robert Coles

In times of crisis, all of us reach for someone or something greater than ourselves. Some call it prayer; others just do it. For many, it's like talking to a wall. The last thing they need is another book that holds out prayer like a good-luck charm.

So instead of theorizing or preaching, Arnold tells stories about real men and women dealing with adversity. Their difficulties – which range from extreme to quite ordinary and universal – will resonate with readers, who will see themselves in these glimpses of anguish, triumph, and peace.

Diane Komp, M.D., author *Breakfast for the Heart*
I love a riveting story that won't go away. That's exactly the type of word picture that Arnold paints, from dark to light, from despair to courage, from pain to joy, from doubt to faith.

Softcover, 200 pages.

Endangered
Your Child in a Hostile World
Johann Christoph Arnold

Don't throw up your hands – you *can* rescue your child. At least that's the advice that Arnold, a father of eight, gives readers in this book. Practical rather than idealistic, *Endangered* takes on an array of contemporary child-rearing issues, from Ritalin and standardized testing to competitiveness and unstructured play. There's also a chapter on the hidden rewards of raising a "difficult" child – a gem that's sure to get chins wagging at home or school. Written for parents (and teachers and caregivers) weary of trying to do the "right" thing, *Endangered* empowers readers to act on the wisdom they already possess.

Library Journal
This is inspiring reading, and not just for parents.

To order: US: **1-800-521-8011** or **724-329-1100**
UK: **0800 018 0799** or **44(0) 1580 88 33 44**
or visit our website: **www.plough.com**